EXPOSITORY WRITING

By Tara McCarthy

SCHOLASTIC
PROFESSIONAL BOOKS

New York • Toronto • London • Auckland • Sydney

Cover design by Vincent Ceci and Jaime Lucero
Interior design by Vincent Ceci and Drew Hires
Interior illustrations by Drew Hires

ISBN 0-590-10387-3

TABLE OF CONTENTS

EXPOSITORY WRITING gives directions, explains a situation or event, or tells how a process happens. It's one of the most formulaic kinds of writing, that is, certain traditional standards are used to write and assess it:

- ✔ **A main idea is clearly stated or implied.**
- ✔ **The main idea is developed and supported by essential facts.**
- ✔ **The facts are presented in a clear, orderly way.**
- ✔ **The presentation is directed toward a specific audience.**

Expository writing is the kind of writing that students are most often asked to do in a school. For example, in history they may write about the sequences of events that lead up to a major event; in science they may write about a process such as metamorphosis; in response to a book they've read, they may tell about its main theme.

In spite of the regular expository writing assignments students are given, they often experience more difficulty with this type of writing than they do with narrative, descriptive, or even persuasive writing. This may be because good expository writing requires more pre-planning, more conscious application of literal thinking skills, and more step-by-step warm-ups, instruction, and practice than do other forms of writing.

This book is designed to help you help students develop the thinking skills and prewriting strategies they need to produce expository writing they will be proud of. The book features:

1. Graduated steps from simpler to more complex forms of expository writing
2. Cross-curricular applications of expository writing skills
3. Opportunities for multi-modal responses
4. On-going review and application
5. Reproducibles that encourage independent learning

Additional Teaching and Learning Ideas

1. Have students write every day.

We learn to write by writing! Though few of us have time to present a formal writing lesson every day, it's usually possible to provide five or ten minutes each day for kids to freewrite on any subject and in whatever mode they wish (e.g., journal entry, poem, news report, story starter, character sketch).

2. Share examples of good expository writing.

Read aloud exemplary models of expository writing that you've come across in your own reading. For example, if you've read a great audience-hooker and main-idea statement in a magazine or in a student's writing, read it aloud to the class, tell why you like it, and encourage student input.

3. Carry out some of the activities in this book on your own and share your insights with your students.

By participating in writing activities, you can help your students understand that learning to write is a lifelong process of discovery and growth. On your own, do some of the activities suggested in this book. After students have done and discussed the activities, tell about the problems and triumphs you encountered. Stress that expository writing isn't always easy to do, but that there's a great reward at the end: a product that states an idea so clearly that the audience says "Wow!"

PART ONE

WRITING MESSAGES, INVITATIONS, AND ANNOUNCEMENTS

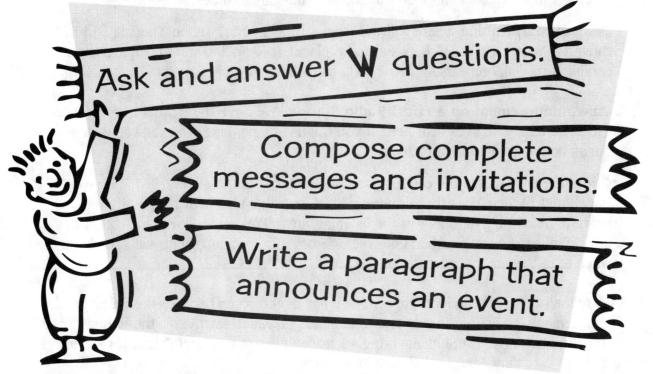

Ask and answer **W** questions.

Compose complete messages and invitations.

Write a paragraph that announces an event.

GETTING STARTED

PREPARATION

For each student, make a copy of *An Invitation* (page 20).

IDEA FOR BUILDING BACKGROUND

Ask students to think back to times when they've received announcements, messages, or invitations, such as an invitation to a party. What information do they expect to get? Examples: what the event is; who is telling about it; when and where the event is taking place. Write students' ideas on the chalkboard.

LISTENING FOR KEY INFORMATION

Ask students to listen as you read the following message and announcements. Tell students that they are to listen for vital information so that they can answer your follow-up

questions. Explain that many of your questions can be answered only by "I don't know" (DK), because the messages are incomplete.

1. A Message on Your Telephone-Answering Machine: Hi! I hope you can come to the Surprise Party! It's happening on Saturday. Don't forget to bring something.

> *Questions:* What kind of party is it? (Surprise) Who left the message? (DK) Whom is the party for? (DK) What day is the party? (Saturday) What time is the party? (DK) Where is the party being held? (DK) What are you supposed to bring? (DK)

2. An Announcement Over the School PA System: School Fair time is almost here! Be sure to have your exhibits ready and make sure you send out your invitations! We'll all get together in the cafeteria at noon this coming Thursday to rehearse.

> *Questions:* When and where will the rehearsal take place? (noon Thursday, in the cafeteria) When will the School Fair take place? (DK) What are students going to exhibit at the Fair? rehearse? (DK) To whom should Fair invitations be sent? (DK)

3. An Announcement on a Local Radio Station: We have the winner in our contest! She's Jane Smith, who lives near here. If you call us in time, Jane, you can come on down to our station and collect your prize.

> *Questions:* What was the contest about? (DK) What is the prize? (DK) Who won? (Jane Smith) Where does the winner live? (DK exactly; just "near here") Might there be more than one Jane Smith in the listening area? (Yes) How does Jane collect her prize? (calls radio station, then goes there) From this announcement, will Jane know when to call/where the radio station is located? (No)

As a follow-up, invite students to act out what might occur because the message and announcements above are incomplete. Examples: (1) Guests arrive at the wrong house for the Surprise Party; (2) Students bring science exhibits to a School Fair about American History; (3) Six "Jane Smiths" call the radio station.

WRITING MESSAGES

Messages are brief, informal notes directed toward a specific person, presented in writing or orally, and usually composed quickly. Informal as they may be, however, good messages clearly state the basic information the recipient needs.

ACTIVITIES

1. Missing Links

On index cards or slips of paper, make two or three copies of the messages in the left-hand column below and distribute them to the class. Explain that the messages are not complete: the person receiving the message needs more information about **what**, **when**,

where, **who**, or **why**. Call on students to read the messages aloud and tell what questions aren't answered. Examples are at the right below.

Messages	What I Need To Know
Please bring the thing from your desk.	**What** thing?
Did you like the other book?	**What** other book?
If I'm not here when they get here, I'll call.	**Who** is "they"? **When** will you call?
Somebody called about the noise.	**Who** is "somebody"? **What** noise?
Be sure to get there on time!	Get **where**? **When** should I get there?
I put the bedroom rug on the porch.	**Why** did you do that?
Mrs. Dupres called. She's upset.	**Why** is she upset? **When** did she call?
I couldn't do one of the chores. I'll do it later.	**What** chore? **When** is "later"?

Next, ask students to rewrite the message they've received so that it briefly answers the questions they've raised. Students can have a lot of fun sharing their rewrites aloud, because each version of the original note will be different. Examples:

Original Message	Sample Rewrites
Please bring the thing from your desk.	• Please bring the secret code from your desk. • Please bring the bologna sandwich from your desk.
Somebody called about the noise.	• Our next-door neighbors called about the loud rock music. • The repair man called about the noise in our new washing machine.

2. Neatness Counts!
Since most messages are still handwritten, here's an opportunity to help students hone their handwriting skills for a practical purpose. Ask students to write their revised messages (above) as neatly as they can. Students can print or use cursive writing. As a challenge,

have students try writing the same message legibly on increasingly smaller pieces of paper. Just for the day, set up a Message Board for displaying these examples of good handwriting.

3. Messages in the Classroom

To help students read and write effective messages, model how to do it by writing personal, pertinent messages to them as real-life occasions arise and ask them to write messages to you. Examples:

> Dolores:
> I liked your story, "Skinny Dog." Would you like to read it aloud to the class this Friday afternoon?
> Ms. Frank

> Ms. Frank:
> I'd like to read "Skinny Dog" next Friday. I want to make some illustrations first.
> Dolores

> Ms. Frank:
> I can't do any homework. It's too noisy where I live.
> Rita

> Rita:
> Let's talk together at lunchtime about your homework. Maybe we can find a way for you do it away from home!
> Ms. Frank

4. Messages at Home and in the Neighborhood

Talk with students about occasions when they think it's important for them to leave a written message for parents or other family members, or for friends and neighbors. As prompts, present the following situations and invite the class to dictate suitable messages.

Write the messages on the chalkboard so that students can revise them.

- You came home from school at the usual time, but you are going to a classmate's home to work on your project for the Science Fair.
- You're responsible for feeding the cats before you leave for school, but there's no cat food left!
- Your friend lost his prized, autographed baseball. You find the baseball at the rec field and put it at your friend's doorstep.

5. 15 Seconds and Out!

You'll need a tape recorder and a stopwatch or a watch with a second hand. Ask students to imagine they've got no more than 15 seconds to leave an important message on a telephone answering machine. The challenge is to tell all the vital information within that time slot.

First, brainstorm about current, local real-life situations or events that are important to your students. Examples:

- A PTA meeting about whether to allot more school-budget money for team sports
- A class book fair to raise money for a class trip
- A public presentation of a video that students have made about local wildlife

Have partners decide on a message to leave on the recipient's answering machine or voice-mail; jot down the basic information the recipient needs to know; use a stopwatch or a watch with a second hand as they practice telling the information in 15 seconds or less. After a couple of practice sessions, partners record the message on tape. The class can listen to several of the recorded messages and comment on strong points.

WRITING INVITATIONS

Writing invitations is an excellent warm-up for doing other kinds of expository writing: invitations are built around a main idea (the event); present facts in a clear, orderly way; and are directed toward a specific audience.

ACTIVITIES

1. Explore a Model

Distribute copies of *An Invitation* (page 20). Go over the instructions with the class and ask students to carry them out. After students compare evaluations, a group spokeperson can summarize the group's ideas for the class.

2. Review Letter Form

Use the invitation on page 20 as a model for discussion of letter form. Ask students to identify the heading, greeting, closing, and signature and to tell where capital letters and commas are used. Point out that the **W** information is in the body of the letter.

COMPOSITION SKILL: ANSWERING W-QUESTIONS

Specific answers to **W-H** questions form the core of most expository writing. In their follow-up discussion of the model invitation on page 20, most students will agree that the invitation answers these basic questions. Students can practice incorporating **W** data into original invitations of their own.

STEPS

1. Brainstorm Have the class brainstorm a chalkboard web that prompts ideas for both realistic and fanciful events. Example:

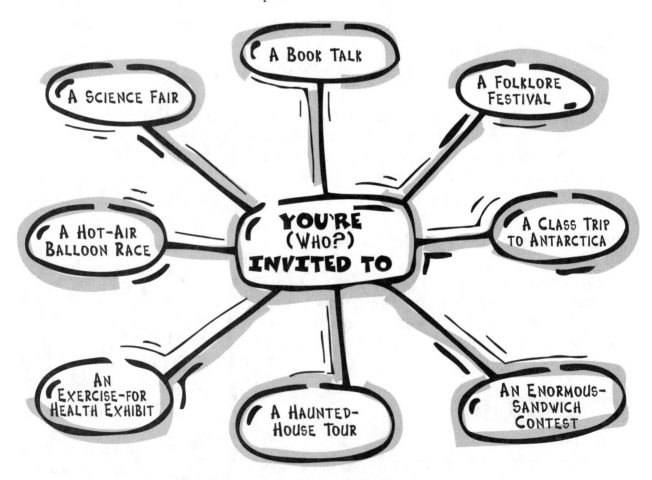

2. Work Together Ask students to work with a partner or in a group of three of four classmates. Students can choose a realistic or fanciful event and write an invitation that gives the necessary **W** information.

3. Plan Suggest that students plan their invitations by first making a five-column chart, one column for each **W** question and its answer.

4. Write One partner or group member can draft the invitation, get revising suggestions from co-writers, and then write a final copy.

5. Deliver, Study, Give Feedback Partners or groups can make copies of their invitation and distribute them to classmates. Classmates read the invitations, determine which **W** questions are answered clearly, and, if necessary, suggest ways to make the invitations more specific.

Well thought-out invitations spark audience attention and encourage positive responses. The following activities help students incorporate fun, audience-grabbing techniques into their original invitations. In implementing the techniques, students will naturally focus on main ideas—a vital focus in all expository writing.

ACTIVITIES

1. Use Visuals
Refer students to the invitations they wrote for the Composition Skill activity (page 11). Invite them to try out pictures, designs, or imaginative lettering that show the main idea or theme of the event. Students might use illuminated capitals or unusual word-processing fonts to emphasize main ideas.

2. Use Exciting Introductions

First, present two ways of opening an invitation. Ask students to determine which way is more exciting, and tell why. Examples:

- We are having a Cultural History Fair. OR You're History, and you can find out why at our Cultural History Fair.
- You're invited to Race! Jump! Throw! Lift!   OR Please come to our physical-fitness exhibit.
- Our class is having a Winter Holiday program. OR On December 3rd, come help us light candles, sing songs, play holiday games, and make gifts.

Then invite the class to compose exciting introductions for invitations to the following events:

- A school celebration of Dr. Martin Luther King's birthday
- A classroom program to celebrate Earth Day
- A welcome-party for new students in your school

3. Combine Strategies

Invite students to use visual devices, an exciting introduction, and basic **W** information to revise an invitation they've already worked on or to design a new invitation.

WRITING PROCESS: AN ANNOUNCEMENT PARAGRAPH

An announcement is an impersonal message directed toward anyone who might be interested in a particular event or situation. Good announcements start by stating the main idea, and follow up with supporting details. That is, they are expository paragraphs.

▶ PREWRITING

1. Present, via copies or on an overhead projector, models of the kinds of announcements students might read on a school or community bulletin board or in a local newspaper. Discuss how the first sentence in each announcement gives the main idea and how the follow-up sentences give details. Point out that an announcement begins with a headline and ends by identifying the writer. Examples:

Dog-Owner Alert

There have been several reports recently about missing dogs. Some lost dogs have ended up in the Animal Shelter. Some stolen dogs have ended up in laboratories and are used for experiments. To keep your dog safe, make sure it has an up-to-date license or an identifying tattoo. Walk your dog on a leash or supervise it during off-leash times. Do not leave your dog alone outside. Report any incidents of missing dogs to the Town Clerk, 555-1900.

Marjorie Ames
Town Clerk

Free Books!

This week after school, from 3:30 to 4:30, there will be a free-books table in the hall outside the school library. The books have been donated by public libraries, by publishers, and by individuals who love reading and love these books in particular. Interested students are invited to select one or two books to take home, enjoy, and keep.

Stan Lesko
School Librarian

2. With the class, work on rephrasing an invitation they've written to turn them into a general announcement. Example:

Animal-Shelter Pet Show

On October 17th from 1 to 2 p.m., Room 10 will present a pet show to raise support for our commmunity's Animal Shelter. All students interested in animal welfare are invited to attend. The show will be held in the gym. Don't bring your real, live pets, but do bring your pictures of and stories about them.

The Room 10 Pet Show Committee

3. With the class, firm up the basic criteria for an announcment:

- The headline, or title, appeals to an audience that would be interested in the event.
- The first sentence of the paragraph states the main idea of the event.
- The rest of the paragraph supplies **W** details that the audience needs to know about the event.
- The writer signs her or his name or the name of the organization.

► DRAFTING AND CONFERENCING

Encourage students to choose announcement subjects that appeal to them. Real-life subjects may include up-coming classroom or school events. Fantasy subjects may be those that resulted from the page 12 brainstorm. After students have written their paragraphs, ask them to confer with a partner to make sure the drafts fulfill the class's criteria for an announcement.

► REVISING AND PROOFREADING

Ask students to work their partner's ideas and their own new views into their drafts. Partners can use word-processor Spell Checks or dictionaries to verify or correct spelling. In addition, you may wish to list three nitty-gritty basics for students to refer to as they proofread:

- Indent the first line of a paragraph.
- Begin each sentence with a capital letter.
- End each sentence with a mark of punctuation.

▶ Publishing Options

1. Students who have written announcements about up-coming, real-life events can reproduce them as flyers to neighbors who might be interested in the event; post them on bulletin boards at school or in local stores; submit them to local newspapers; use them on Internet community-news pages; voice-mail them to locals who might be interested in the event.

2. Students who have written announcements about fantasy events can anthologize the announcements in a class Story Ideas folder, put them in their personal writer-journals as story-starter perks, or add them to their portfolios to show how they're learning about the five **W**'s.

3. Invite students to get together and plan and present a radio or TV news show that includes announcements about real-life events along with announcements about fantasy events. Have students set up criteria for each reporter. For example: (1) Keep a straight face. (2) Include all the vital **W** data.

ACROSS THE CURRICULUM

1. History: An Invitation to a Long-Ago Event

Have students brainstorm a list of important historical events they've learned about. Then ask partners or small groups to choose one of the events and "go back in time," imagining that the event is just about to happen. Students can then write invitations to the event. Example:

June 4, 1776

Dear Patriot,
　　Mark July 4, 1776, on Your Must-Be-There calendar!
Come to Independence Hall in Philadelphia to witness the
signing of the Declaration of Independence. You won't
want to miss this event, because it will free us from
English rule of the colonies.
　　　　　　　　　Sincerely,
　　　　　　　　　[Student's name]

2. Literature: An Announcement About a Book Character

Discuss with students some of the literary characters they admire. Examples: Charlotte, of *Charlotte's Web*, saves a friend by writing wonderful messages in her web. Stuart, of *Stuart Little*, defeats odds by sailing a boat to victory on a pond. Adam, of *Adam of the Road*, overcomes dangers and finds his dad. Then ask students to imagine that one of these characters has come alive and will visit your school to tell about her or his adventure. Partners can then write an announcement of the event. Example:

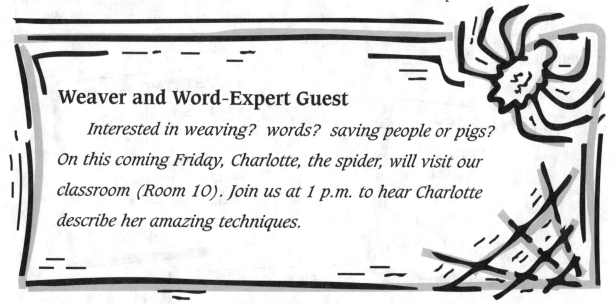

Weaver and Word-Expert Guest

Interested in weaving? words? saving people or pigs?
On this coming Friday, Charlotte, the spider, will visit our
classroom (Room 10). Join us at 1 p.m. to hear Charlotte
describe her amazing techniques.

3. Science: A Message to and from a Scientist

Ask students to imagine that they are assistants to reknowned scientists whose work they've studied in class. What questions might they have as their employers pursue an experiment or idea? Invite students to write their questions as informal messages. Examples:

Mr. Hubbel:
I'm confused. Exactly what is this
telescope supposed to do?

Mr. Bell:
I like your communication device!
What are you going to call it?

Ask partners to exchange messages and answer them via a message from the "boss." Partners can then read their messages aloud to the class. The audience should listen to determine if the question is clear and if the answer is correct.

WORKPLACE SKILL: WRITING CLASSIFIED ADS

From local newspapers, clip classified advertisements that appear under Help Wanted, Lost and Found, Pets, and Personals. Distribute copies of the ads or show them on an overhead projector. Examples:

LOST AND FOUND

Lost: Silver ring with amethyst, near Woodstock fairground June 2. Sentimental value. Reward. Call 212-555-7836.

HELP WANTED

Gardener: Four hours weekly. Mow, weed, rake, plant. Must be self-starter. Call 555-7878. Days and pay negotiable.

PETS

Adorable Akita: One-year-old female. Neutered, all shots. Can't move her to apartment. Loves kids, exercise. Responsible parties only. Call 555-0103.

Discuss with students the main idea that's summarized in the newspaper headings. For example: **(PETS) Here's some information about pets. (HELP WANTED) Here are some job opportunities.** Explain that people who place classified ads under these headings are charged by the word. Typically (and for the activities that follow), $30 for the first 20 words; $1 for each additional word; hyphenated words count as two words; phone numbers count as one word.

Assign students to count the number of words in each example and to determine (1) what the ad-placer must pay (for example, the Help Wanted ad has 18 words, so the advertiser pays $30; the Personal ad has 25 words, so the advertiser pays $35); and (2) how many words the advertiser might add or try to delete from the ad to come in exactly at the $30 fee (for example, the Lost and Found ad could add five words; the Pets ad would have to delete two words).

Ask students to record their tabulations on a chalkboard chart. Have the class suggest how they might add to or subtract from the ads.

School Applications

Set up a classroom or school classified ads bulletin board where students can post brief ads under main-idea headings. For starters: Lost and Found, Wanted, For Sale, Personals. Each ad should be dated. Each week, assign three or four students to collect and post new ads and to remove those that have received responses or that have been posted for more than a month.

Lost and Found

Lost: On rec field. Key on blue plastic ring. See Lyn, Room 156.
Post Date: 10/2

FOR SALE

Ice-skates, size 9. Black, hardly worn at all. Call Barry, 555-0978. $25 or best offer.
Post date: 10/18

Wanted

Used toys for Holiday Toy Drive. Must be in good condition. Bring to Youth Center between 3 and 8 p.m.
Post date: 11/12

Names _____ _____

AN INVITATION
Presenting the Five W's

With your partner, read the invitation. Then do the activity below it.

October 8, 1998

Dear Families,

   The students of Room 10 at Eberley School invite you to our Pet Show. It will be held in the gymnasium on October 17th, from 1 p.m. to 2 p.m. The purpose of our show is to raise support for the Animal Shelter. But the show will be unusual, because no actual pets will be here. Instead, we'll use costumes, plays, poems, and pictures to tell you about our real pets and about pets we'd like to have! We hope you'll join us for this fun-filled event.

Sincerely,

Jaime Duque

Chairman, Pet Show Committee

Use the invitation above to answer the questions.

WHO is giving the Pet Show? _____

WHEN will the show take place? _____

WHERE will the show take place? _____

WHY is the Pet Show being given? _____

WHAT will be unusual or special about the show? _____

Make a check in the box that shows your evaluation of the invitation.

☐ Excellent   ☐ Good   ☐ Fair   ☐ Poor

With a group of classmates, compare evaluations. Give reasons for your evaluation.

PART TWO

WRITING DIRECTIONS AND EXPLANATIONS

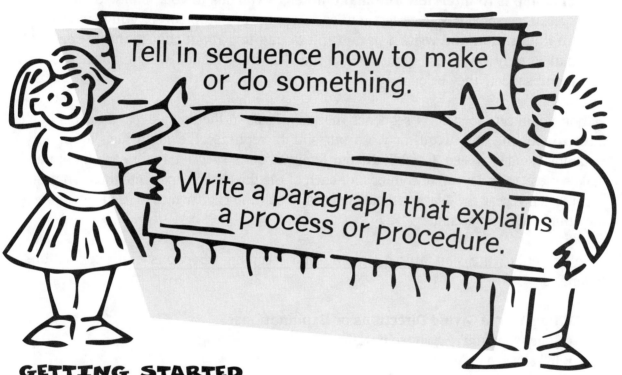

Tell in sequence how to make or do something.

Write a paragraph that explains a process or procedure.

GETTING STARTED

PREPARATION

For each student, make a copy of *Family Festival Calendar* (page 35) and *Directions for an ET* (page 37).

IDEA FOR BUILDING BACKGROUND

Briefly brainstorm out-of-school situations in which it's important to follow oral or written directions. Some examples are: in fire or medical emergencies, in playing games and sports, in filling out job forms, in telling or finding out how to get from one place to another. Ask students why manufacturers include directions or explanations on drugstore items, packaged or frozen foods, power tools, and home appliances, and on electronic devices such as VCR's, word processors, and cell phones. You may invite students to bring to class examples of directions and instructions that accompany such products. Which are clear? Which are confusing? Why?

LISTENING FOR STEPS

Explain to students that you'll read aloud the directions for making a Family Festival Calendar; that there are three main steps; that students are to listen carefully for the main idea in each step; that when you've finished reading, you'll ask students to summarize the three steps in order.

Teacher Read-Aloud (Stress the boldfaced phrases.)

Here's how to make a Family Festival Calendar. **Step one is to get your supplies together.** You'll need a free, illustrated, month-by-month calendar from a local store or business; 12 pieces of paper big enough to cover over the pictures on the calendar; paste or glue; colored markers, crayons, and pencils. **The second step is to interview and make notes** as you talk to your family to find a special, personal day to celebrate in each month. **For step three, you'll make an illustration and write a paragraph or caption about that month's special Family Day.** Paste your new calendar illustrations and writing above the months where they belong.

Call on volunteers to state in sequence the main ideas in the three steps. Students don't have to say the step word-for-word but simply rephrase the main idea accurately. (Example, student's Step 2: " Talk to your family about a special day for each month and make notes.") Get several rewordings for each of the three steps and write them on poster paper. Then repeat the Teacher Read-Aloud and ask the class which student rewordings they think are most accurate.

Help students write standards for giving and receiving directions and explanations. Examples:

When You're Giving Directions or Explanations:
- State what you're going to explain.
- Tell steps in order.
- Include all the essential information.
- Leave out details that aren't necessary.

When You're Reading or Listening to Directions or Explanations:
- Read or listen for the main steps.
- Remember the sequence of the steps.
- If possible, ask questions about steps or details that aren't clear to you.

COMPLETING DIRECTIONS

Distribute the copies of *Family Festival Calendar* (page 35). Preview the instructions with the class and have students carry them out independently or with a partner. Invite students to make Festival Calendars of their own.

COMPOSITION SKILL: STATING THE SEQUENCE

Most students are familiar with visual ways of indicating the sequence. For example: numerals preceding each step, icons (•••, ✔✔✔, ◆◆◆), paragraph indents to signal new steps. You may wish to review these visual devices with students before moving them on to reviewing verbal step-signals.

1. Review Sequence Words and Phrases

Ahead of time, make lists of out-of-order sequence words. Provide space on each list for student rewrites. Example lists:

Second _____	Finally _____	Start by _____	Next _____
Third _____	First _____	Last _____	Begin by _____
First _____	Next _____	Then _____	End by _____

After that _____	Finish by _____
Step one is _____	Now _____
To complete _____	Start by _____
Step two is _____	The third step is _____

Distribute lists to partners. Partners have 30 seconds maximum to rewrite their list to show the time-order sequence correctly—for example, Start by, Now, The third step is, Finish by.

To check whether their rewritten lists are correct, ask partners to use the list to call out directions (not demonstrate) to a small group of classmates in an improvised, physical exercise. Example:

> Start by standing up straight. Now touch your toes without bending your knees. The third step is to move your arms from side to side like an elephant swinging its trunk. Finish by standing up straight again and taking a deep breath.

Ask the audience to name the sequence words that helped them do the exercise and to comment on sequence words that seemed to be out of order. Suggest that partners use classmates' input and their own ideas to write the final directions. Students may record the directions for a tape-anthology of Bad-Weather, No-Playground, Indoor-Exercises.

2. Put Directions in Order: Getting to a Place

On an overhead projector, show the map and paragraph on page 36. Before you or a student reads the paragraph to the class, explain that it is an example of how not to give directions. After reading, ask students why the directions are confusing. (Examples: Steps are not given in order. Some important information is missing, such as whether to turn left or right. The directions don't say which house on Birch Lane is Leonard's).

Ask partners or groups of three or four students to use the map and the results of the class discussion to write clear directions for getting to Leonard's house. Results will vary slightly but should show a grasp of sequence and an attention to detail. To check out the accuracy of directions, classmates can study the map as they listen to one of the writers read the directions aloud. Example:

> ### *Directions to Leonard's Birthday Party*
> *Travel west on Route 9 until you get to Main Street. Turn left on Main Street.*
> *Go to the second traffic light. This is Birch Lane. Turn right on Birch Lane.*
> *Look for the Quick-Stoppie on your left. Leonard's house, #7 Birch Lane, is*
> *directly across the street on your right.*

3. Provide Directions for an ET!

Distribute the copies of *Directions for an ET* (page 37) and preview the situation and the task. If necessary, briefly review the strategies students have learned: (1) tell steps in order, (2) use sequence words where they'd be helpful. Call attention to the last prompt on the page. A classmate will play the part of the ET and follow the directions exactly as presented. Writers may then have to add to or clarify steps in their directions.

CREATING VISUALS

Written directions and explanations are often accompanied by pictures and diagrams. In addition, some information and directions can be supplied by symbols or pictures alone. Students can learn to incorporate clear-cut visuals into many of the directions they compose. In doing so, students develop their ability to stick to essentials, to use time-order sequence, and to consider the needs of the audience.

To set the stage and elicit background knowledge, display some common visuals such as maps, the directions folders enclosed with tools and electronic equipment, or the icons or small drawings often accompanying packaged meals. You may also wish to reproduce some of the international signs shown on this page. Briefly discuss with the class why the visuals are useful. Ask students to bring to class and share other examples of pictures and symbols that give directions. Instead, they may translate the icons that appear on word processors.

ACTIVITIES

1. Make Pictures-Only Directions

Ask students to work independently or with a partner to make pictures-only signs that give directions. Some examples are: Do Not Touch, Open—Please Come In, Watch Your Step, No Swimming, Flowers for Sale, No Hitchhiking, Use Other Door. Have partners show their signs to classmates, ask for verbal translations, then, if necessary, revise the signs to make them clearer. This is an excellent opportunity for ESL students to work with English-dominant classmates to come up with signs that are comprehensible to a wide audience.

As a follow-up, students may discuss where pictures-only directions might be useful in and around the classroom, school, or neighborhood; design the signs; and post them (with appropriate permission, of course). Examples:

Don't pick the flowers.

Cafeteria is this way.

Art Show is this way.

Watch your step.

2. Make Step-by-Step Drawings and Captions

Have students name favorite holidays and family/cultural celebrations, then lead into a discussion of special decorations that go with the festivities. Ask partners to choose one of the decorations and make a captioned picture-panel that tells how to make it. Review the criteria for directions: clarity, accuracy, completeness, brevity, time-order sequence. You may wish to show the example that follows.

HOW TO MAKE LUMINARIOS

1. For each light, you'll need: a small brown bag; about 2 cups of fine, clean sand; a stubby votive candle; a match.

2. Put the sand in the bag.

3. Stick the candle firmly in the sand.

4. Place your luminarios outside. Light the candles!

EXPLANATIONS

Directions tell how to carry out a process, e.g., prepare the meal, find the party site, make the holiday decoration. **Explanations** are directed toward an audience that wishes to understand a process. In school, students are often asked to write explanations of a process in nature, such as the metamorphosis of an insect or of how a discovery was made, such as Newton's discovery of the law of gravity. Good explanations, like good directions, present steps in time-sequence. Students who have begun to master the skill of giving accurate directions can move on to writing concise explanations.

ACTIVITIES

1. Analyze a Model

Via an overhead projector on the chalkboard, present the following paragraph and use these questions to help students explore it:

- What does the paragraph explain? (why Columbus thought America was India, why native inhabitants of America were called "Indians" by Columbus and other Europeans)
- Where is the main idea stated? (in the title, in the first sentence)
- What are some words and phrases that help you follow the explanation step by step? (Examples are underlined in the paragraph.)

BIG DISCOVERY, WRONG NAME!

Columbus made a big discovery by mistake and named people by mistake. Here's how it happened. Knowing that the world was round, Columbus started out from Europe to find a westward route to Asia and India. After many hard months sailing west, Columbus and his crew indeed reached land. "This must be India!" they decided. So when they encountered the native peoples, they called them "Indians." Before long, Columbus and other Europeans realized that the little fleet had come ashore on a gigantic continent—America—they had not known existed. But even after that, the word "Indians" stuck as a name for Native Americans.

2. Complete an Explanation

Ask students to study the following paragraph together and then (1) choose the opening (topic) sentence that sums up the main idea, (2) select the words or phrases that make the time sequence clear, and (3) choose the title that gives the main idea. (Correct answers are underlined.) Along the way, as students select words and phrases, have them read the sentences aloud so that they can hear how time-sequence connectives can make an explanation clear.

TITLE
- How to Raise Potatoes
- How Hunger Brought the Irish to America
- How the English Farmed Land in Their Colonies

OPENING SENTENCE
- During the 1840s, thousands of Irish families came to America.
- Immigrants usually find it difficult to adjust to a new home.
- All over the world, farmers work to use crop lands in wise ways.

They were fleeing from the Great Famine, or Great Hunger. Potatoes (are now, <u>had long been</u>) the main food source for Irish tenant farmers. (<u>When,</u> After that) A disease, or potato-blight, rotted the potato crop several years in a row, tenant farmers ran short of food. (Eventually, <u>As usual</u>) The English landlords in Ireland kept on sending other food crops to England. Irish farmers were starving. (Before that, <u>Soon</u>) Hungry Irish families had shipped out to Canada and to the United States in the hope of finding a new place to survive.

- What other important processes could you explain to an audience by using pictures and time-sequence words?

WRITING PROCESS:
A PARAGRAPH THAT DIRECTS OR EXPLAINS

Directions and explanations are alike in that they present a procedure step-by-step. This step-by-step facet is the one you'll want students to focus on, whether they choose to write a direction paragraph or an explanation paragraph.

▶ PREWRITING
1. Present, via copies or on an overhead projector, examples of how "my dog ate my homework" can be presented either as directions or as explanation. Discuss how both examples follow a time sequence.

Explanation:

Why My Dog Is Responsible for My Missing Homework
Here's why I don't have my history report to hand in. I did write the report. Then I put it on the kitchen table. My dog Fritz, who hadn't eaten since breakfast, was very hungry. He smelled a glob of peanut butter on the table. Fritz put his front paws on the table to get at the peanut butter. After eating the peanut butter, Fritz went right on to eat other things on the table, including my wonderful history report.

Directions:

How to Get Your Dog to Eat Your Homework
First, spread globs of peanut butter on your homework report. Second, put your peanut-buttered report on the floor. Then, call your dog and direct her or his attention to the interesting yummy item. Finally, praise your dog as she or he eats your homework.

2. Via a chalkboard chart, list some topics, both realistic and fanciful, that can be developed either through directions or explanations. Provide and discuss some example titles, as shown. Invite students to suggest titles for the other topics. (Possibilities are underlined.)

TOPIC	TITLE FOR DIRECTIONS	TITLE FOR EXPLANATION
Playing a Word Game	How to Play Scrabble	How I Win Scrabble Games
Planning a Family Vacation	Map Skills for Vacationers	How Our Map—and WE— Got Lost!
Studying Wild Birds	How to Tally Birds at a Bird Feeder	What Happens to Birds as Woodlands Are Destroyed
Attending a Birthday Party	Directions to Samantha's House	How Faulty Directions Ended Me Up on the Planet Mars

3. Briefly review with the class the criteria for giving explanations and directions (page 22). If necessary, work with the class to compose a paragraph of directions or explanation for one of the chart entries.

4. Ask students to get together with three or four classmates to list topics they're all fairly familiar with, such as the topics on the foregoing chart. Other examples of topics are: A Class Field Trip, Presenting a Play, A School Athletic Event, A Program for Parents, A Library Display, A Special Classroom Visitor, A "Snow-Day" Emergency, A Fund-Raising Event.

▶ **DRAFTING**
Ask students to choose one of the topics they've discussed and write a paragraph that either gives directions for carrying out an activity or that explains how something happened. Remind students to keep steps in time-order and to use helpful time-order words and phrases. For reference, students can use the time-order lists on page 23.

► CONFERENCING

On the chalkboard or on poster paper, copy the following chart and suggest that partners use it as they study and discuss one another's drafts.

DIRECTING AND EXPLAINING

	Yes	No	Suggestions
1. You stated the main topic in the title and/or in the first sentence.			
2. You told about events in the order they happened.			
3. You told all the important steps.			
4. Everything you said relates to the main topic.			
5. You used helpful time-sequence words and phrases.			

► REVISING

Suggest that students use three revision steps:

1. Use your partner's suggestions and your own ideas to write a second draft of your paragraph.

2. Ask your partner to listen as you read your second draft aloud. Then ask your partner to repeat the directions or explanation in her or his own words.

3. Use your partner's retelling to decide if your paragraph is as clear as you can make it. If necessary, make some final revisions.

► PROOFREADING

1. Briefly review the proofreading steps on page 15 and ask students to implement them as they make final copies of their paragraphs.

2. You may wish to introduce or review accepted form for writing titles. As the safest bet for all students, ask that all words in a title be capitalized.

► PUBLISHING OPTIONS

1. Ask a group of four or five students to study classmates' completed paragraphs and then to organize them in categories for a Sample Directions and Explanations Reference

Anthology for all students to use as they prepare for various assignments and tests. Categories can be wide and general, for example:

- Part 1: Good Examples of Directions for How to Do Something
- Part 2: Good Examples of Explaining How Something Happens

Or, compilers may think of other categories, for example:

- Using Pictures to Direct and Explain
- Using Helpful Sequence Words
- Presenting Ideas in Order
- Strong Titles and Opening Sentences

2. For families at home, students can compile a Writing Bulletin that sums up what the class has learned about writing directions and explanations. (This is an excellent opportunity for fostering metacognition, that is, for focusing on the thought-processes that underlie a writing product.) Procedure:

- At the chalkboard, work with the class to write an introduction for their Bulletin.
- The first part of the introduction should define *explanation* and *directions*, and then tell how the two forms are alike. Example:

> **DIRECTIONS** tell you how to do something. **EXPLANATIONS** tell you how something happened. Directions and explanations are alike because they tell all the important steps and tell them in order.

- The second part of the introduction should sum up some of the activities that helped students learn how to write directions and explanations. Example:

> To learn how to write directions and explanations, we listened to good examples. We wrote directions for getting from one place to another and for making holiday decorations. We wrote explanations of historical events and of science phenomena. We learned how to use sequence words and helpful pictures to make directions and explanations clear.

A class committee can choose from the final writing products three or four good examples of directions and three or four explanations to include in the Writing Bulletin under a general heading such as SOME EXAMPLES OF OUR BEST WORK. Another committee can organize the Bulletin and reproduce copies for distribution.

ACROSS THE CURRICULUM

1. Geography: Explaining How to Use an Atlas

Have on hand three or four different atlases. Each student works with a partner or small group to explore one of the atlases. After discussing the general organization of the atlas, partners or groups decide on a "How To..." topic that they can explain orally to classmates. Examples:

How to Use This Atlas to...

- Find the exact location of a city in a distant country.
- Figure out what clothes to take on a July vacation to (a place far from home).
- Locate the three highest mountains in the world/deepest parts of the world's oceans/places with the warmest and coolest average temperatures/longest rivers/heaviest yearly rainfall.
- Determine the shortest air route from New York City to Thailand.
- See how maps have changed over the centuries.
- Figure out two or three places where crops can be grown all year round.

Partners/groups practice their oral presentations. Suggest that (1) the presentation start with a statement of what will be explained and (2) presenters use sequence words and phrases, and show specific atlas pages as they point to relevant features. Conclude with a class discussion: What was best about each presentation? What could have been made clearer? What did the audience learn about the contents of atlases? How can they use their new knowledge to help them in their work at school?

2. Writing: Addressing Different Audiences

You can help students adjust their directions and explanations according to the audience they're addressing. Suggested procedure:

* Have students brainstorm to complete a chalkboard web about Hot Topics they've recently studied in various curricular areas. Example:

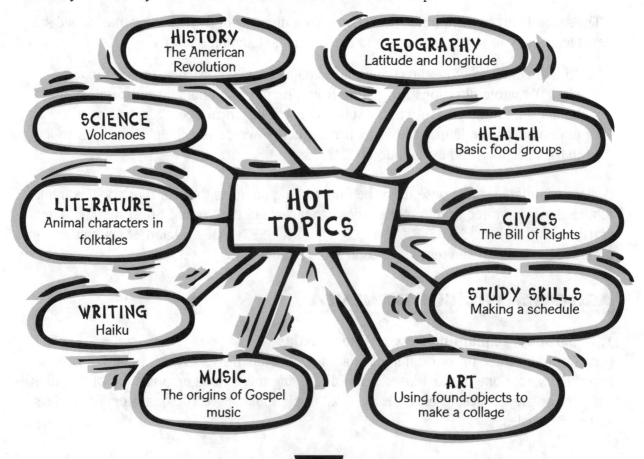

HISTORY The American Revolution

GEOGRAPHY Latitude and longitude

SCIENCE Volcanoes

HEALTH Basic food groups

LITERATURE Animal characters in folktales

HOT TOPICS

CIVICS The Bill of Rights

WRITING Haiku

STUDY SKILLS Making a schedule

MUSIC The origins of Gospel music

ART Using found-objects to make a collage

Ask partners to choose from the chalkboard web the Hot Topic that most interests them and that they feel they know a lot about. Then ask students to imagine three different audiences:

1. Younger students in your school who know little or nothing about the subject
2. Families-at-home who know something about the topic, but maybe not as much as you do
3. Classmates who have studied the topic with you but who may welcome additional information or clarification

Have partners choose one of the three audiences, outline a presentation of the topic, then make the presentations to the selected audience. Back in class, partners can report what they've learned about the audience. Example:

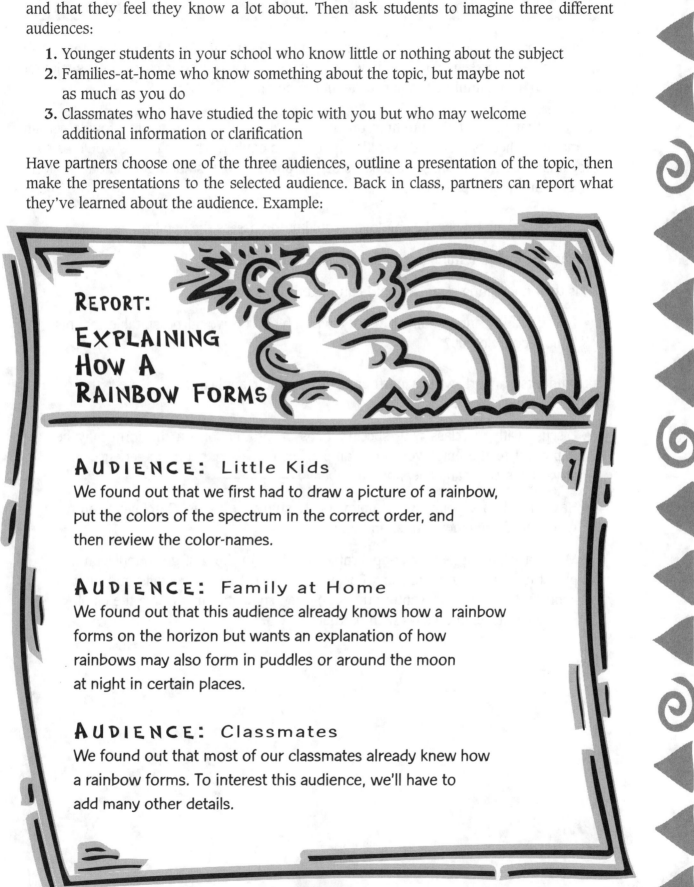

REPORT:
EXPLAINING
HOW A
RAINBOW FORMS

AUDIENCE: Little Kids
We found out that we first had to draw a picture of a rainbow, put the colors of the spectrum in the correct order, and then review the color-names.

AUDIENCE: Family at Home
We found out that this audience already knows how a rainbow forms on the horizon but wants an explanation of how rainbows may also form in puddles or around the moon at night in certain places.

AUDIENCE: Classmates
We found out that most of our classmates already knew how a rainbow forms. To interest this audience, we'll have to add many other details.

WORKPLACE SKILL:
FILLING OUT AN EMPLOYMENT APPLICATION

Distribute copies of the *Employment Application* form on page 38. Explain that forms like these are usually presented to people who want certain jobs—in this case a job as a junior counselor in a community Summer Recreation program.

Point out that most of the prompts on the form direct the applicant to provide certain information, whereas prompt 8 asks the applicant to explain why he or she would be suited for this job. After reading and discussing the prompts, ask students to fill out the form independently (using pencil).

Next, present some rubrics the employer would use to assess the applicants:

- Has the applicant fully given all the information asked for?

- Is the handwriting clear, so that I can read the answers?

- Has the applicant explained exactly why she or he would be suitable for this junior-counselor job?

Ask students to work with a partner to revise their applications to meet the rubrics. To conclude the activity:

- Discuss with the class why specific items of information on the form may be important to the employer, for example, references, previous experience, and physician's name and telephone number.

- Have the class appoint two "employers" to study the forms. Employers can tell which applicants they'd hire, and why.

- Model a follow-up employer-applicant interview. In the first go-round, you can play the role of the employer. (For example, ask for more details and discuss applicant's reasons for wanting the job.) Then students can assume the employer role for model interviews with partners.

Names _____

FAMILY FESTIVAL CALENDAR

June 22nd is GEBERT ARRIVAL DAY! On that day in 1937, my great-grand-parents Naomi and Sol Gebert came to New York from Germany. Two years later, they became American citizens.

JUNE 1998

S	M	T	W	T	F	S
	1	2	3	4	5	6
7	8	9	10	11	12	13
14	15	16	17	18	19	20
21	(22)	23	24	25	26	27
28	29	30				

In pencil, write the directions for making a Family Festival Calendar.

1. Supplies _____

_____

_____

2. Find out _____

_____

_____

3. Make the calendar by _____

Share and discuss your directions with some classmates. Find strong points and weak points. Then, if necessary, revise your directions.

DIRECTIONS TO LEONARD'S BIRTHDAY PARTY

When you get to a traffic light, turn on Birch Lane. But before that, go along on Main Street to a stoplight. You follow Route 9 East to get to Main Street. Then turn. A landmark on Birch Lane is the Quick-Stoppie Shop-and-Stop. Leonard's house is on Birch Lane, too.

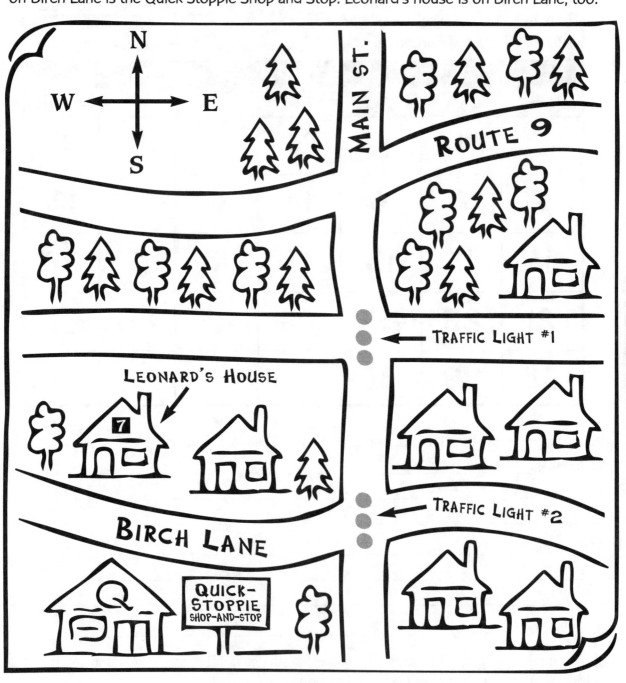

Name _____

DIRECTIONS FOR AN ET

The ET is highly intelligent, understands English, but is unfamiliar with basic tasks you or other Earthlings do every day.

1. Choose and copy one of the ET's questions. Write directions to answer it.

> How do you make a peanut-butter sandwich?

> How do you work a tape recorder?

> What should I do when the fire-drill bell rings?

ET's QUESTION: _____

_____

Our Directions, Step by Step: _____

_____

_____

_____

_____

_____

2. Ask a classmate to play the part of the ET. Read your directions to the actor and ask her or him to follow your directions exactly.

3. Did everything go right? Why or why not?

4. If necessary, rewrite your directions to make them absolutely clear. Test your revision by asking another ET actor to follow it.

EMPLOYMENT APPLICATION

Position: *Junior Counselor*, Summer Recreation Program

Today's Date: _____

1. Name _____ M _____ F _____

2. Home Address: _____

   Street _____ Town/City _____ ZIP _____

3. Home Telephone: _____

4. Parent or Guardian: _____ Telephone at Work: _____

5. Your Birthdate: Month _____ Day _____ Year _____

6. School Information: Name of Your School: _____

   Grade you will have completed: _____ Your teacher's name: _____

7. Your doctor's name: _____ Phone #: _____

8. Briefly explain what experience you've had in working with
   children ages 5–8. Use the back of this page if you need extra space. _____

   _____

9. Check the three skills that you think are your strongest:

   Softball _____   Nature Study _____   Music _____

   Story-Hour _____   Food Preparation _____   Swimming _____

   Hiking and Camping Out _____   Organizing Games _____

10. **REFERENCES:** On the back of this page, list at least three references—people we can
    contact who will tell us about your qualifications for this job. Supply full name, address,
    and phone number for each reference.

PART THREE

WRITING EXPOSITORY PARAGRAPHS

Identify and state main ideas.

Write topic sentences.

Develop main ideas in different ways.

GETTING STARTED

PREPARATION

For each student, make copies of pages 57–60 (four ways of developing main ideas) and of page 63 (Our Group-Plans Paragraphs). For the Building Background activity, have on hand a variety of newspapers and periodicals.

IDEA FOR BUILDING BACKGROUND

Distribute the newspapers/periodicals and explain the initial task: Students will have two minutes to scan the material to find the one article they'd read first and to write the title, or headline, of the article. Call on students to tell why they chose the particular article. Expect and encourage a variety of responses (e.g., love the subject, attention-grabbing picture, dramatic headline, weird subject, relates to a school subject, about a local event that affects me, subject often discussed at home, looks easy to read).

Next, ask three or four students to read the headlines of their articles. Write the headlines on the chalkboard and ask the class to brainstorm questions that they would expect to be answered in the articles. Examples:

BATTLE OF THE BUDGETS: MAYOR FIGHTS SCHOOL BOARD
What is the battle of the budgets about? What does the mayor want? What does the school board want? How does the battle affect kids and teachers?

LOCAL CHAMP WOWS INTERNATIONAL AUDIENCE
Who is the local champ? What is she or he a champion at? How did she or he "wow" an audience? Where and when did the event take place?

CAN THIS RAP STAR SUCCEED IN A NEW FIELD?
Who is the rap star? What's the new field? Why does the star want to be in this new field?

Discuss with the class: A good headline states the main idea of an article. Students have chosen many headlines and have many questions to ask about the subject. What's the responsibility of the article writer? (to answer the readers' questions) Some students may wish to read the articles in their entirety and tell the class how well the writers met this responsibility.

LISTENING FOR THE MAIN IDEA

Write these headlines on the chalkboard:

TRAINING YOUR DOG   MY FAVORITE DOG   CHOOSING A PUPPY
GOOD WATCH DOGS   ADVENTURES WITH DOGS   DOG INTELLIGENCE

Explain the task:
- You're going to read a paragraph that states the main idea at the beginning and at the end.
- Students are to listen so that they can choose the headline that best suits the paragraph (Choosing a Puppy).
- They are to state the main idea in a sentence of their own.
- Students should restate at least two facts or examples that support the main idea.

You may wish to duplicate and distribute the paragraph for follow-up discussion.

Teacher Read-Aloud
When it comes to selecting a dog as a pet, you have to consider the characteristics and needs of different dogs, and your characteristics, too! Some breeds of dogs, like Cairn and Jack Russell terriers, are lively and yappy and need lots of play-time with their owners. Other dogs, like German shepherds and rottweilers, are happiest as guard dogs, protecting their human families from real or imagined dangers. Dogs like collies, setters, retrievers, hounds, and huskies

require long periods of exercise in big, open fields. And then there are some couch-potato dogs, like the tiny Yorkie or the huge Bernese mountain dog, that are content just hanging-out around the house with couch-potato people. So, when you're considering a puppy, think hard about how its natural personality is going to fit in with yours.

As a metacognition follow-up, ask students why the discarded titles are not appropriate.

USING WHAT YOU KNOW

Identifying main ideas and supporting facts in professional articles is an important first step for young writers. The next step is to center on and develop a main idea of one's own.

ACTIVITIES

1. It's All in Your Head!
Prepare several sheets of noteboook paper with a very broad subject written at the top of each. Include subjects that are unusual or fun. (See examples below.) Place the pages subject-side down.

Sample Subjects

birds	homes	planets	forests	holidays
clothes	music	sports	planes	shopping malls
food	fear	money	colors	weather
friends	jobs	dinosaurs	school	books

Ask students to work with one or two classmates. Partners select a page at random, then brainstorm and write on it as many words and phrases as possible that pop into their heads about the subject. Stress that there's a time limit (your choice—five minutes max.) and that there isn't any "right" or "wrong" for this activity. The object is to make as long a list as possible. You may want to first provide a fast warm-up, via a whole-class brainstorm, about one of the subjects. Write responses on the chalkboard. Add some of your own ideas, if you wish.

Broad Subject: Music

Rap Artists	Music videos	Guitars	Drums	Sad Music
Music I Love	Music I Hate	Lyrics	Radios	Music Lessons
Earphones	Making Up Songs	Concerts	Rhythm	
Dancing	Bands	Rock stars	Holiday Music	

Next, ask students to circle on their lists the four or five items that interest them most and that they'd like to find out more about. Ask groups to keep their lists to use soon. (See Activity 2, following.)

2. Brainstorm for Main Ideas

On the chalkboard, list some items that groups circled for Activity 1. Ask the class to brainstorm for a main idea about each item. Stress that the main idea should be stated as a complete sentence (a statement or a question). Encourage students to build on their own interest in or prior knowledge about a subject. Examples:

Favorite Item	Main Idea
Music I Love	There are certain kinds of music I could listen to all day long.
Basketball	Who thought up the game of basketball?
Tornadoes	How does a tornado form?
Exploring Mars	The space-probe of Mars resulted in valuable knowledge about our solar system.

Ask students to work with their partners again to compose main idea statements or questions about other items they circled on their lists.

DEVELOPING A MAIN IDEA

There are four traditional ways to develop a main idea in an expository paragraph:

- examples
- comparison and contrast
- cause and effect
- definition and explanation

ACTIVITIES

1. Explore Strategies One-by-One

To help students learn, review, or practice each strategy, you can use the following sequence with any of the reproducibles on pages 57–60.

- Distribute copies of the page. Read the title, and the heading, words and phrases in the box. Preview the prompts that students are to respond to. Students work independently or with a partner to complete the page.
- Invite students to share their responses with a group or with the whole class.

2. Apply the Strategies

Almost any subject can be approached through different expository strategies, depending on the writer's purpose. For example, the subject Team Sports can be developed by giving examples or by comparing and contrasting team sports with one-on-one sports such as tennis. The subject Tornadoes can be developed by defining and explaining what a tornado is, or by telling how a tornado affects areas where it touches down. To help students apply different expository strategies, display the page 62 visual on an overhead projector and discuss it with the class. Students can then work with three of four classmates to draw and complete a similar web based on a subject of their own choosing.

FOCUS ON BEGINNING

For most writers, just getting started is the hardest part of writing: to coax from oneself that first sentence. You must remember that it doesn't have to be "perfect" and can always be changed in part or entirely at any point in the writing process. You can use the two activities that follow to encourage students to "just begin."

ACTIVITIES

1. Develop a Purpose Statement
A writer's purpose statement is a guideline for the writer alone. The statement seldom appears as such in the final piece of expository writing. Rather, it serves as a compass-point to help writers decide exactly what it is they want to tell about and to keep them on target as they select details to include in their paragraph.

To help students develop an idea of what a purpose statement is, write groups of statements on the chalkboard and ask students to tell which statement or statements are exact and which aren't. Examples:

- My purpose is to tell about bats.
- My purpose is to tell how bats can free areas of insects.
- My purpose is to tell about hurricanes.
- My purpose is to explain what causes a hurricane to form.
- My purpose is to tell how meterologists track hurricanes.
- My purpose is to give examples of dog intelligence.
- My purpose is to tell about dogs.
- My purpose is to compare and contrast two breeds of dogs.

Most students will readily identify the vague "tell about's" as not being exact. With the class, discuss how an exact purpose statement will help a writer decide on the right set of facts to use in a paragraph. Encourage students to write clear, exact purpose statements to guide them as they work on their paragraphs.

2. Develop a Topic Sentence

A good topic sentence is like a headline: It clearly states the writer's main idea, and it appears at, or very near, the beginning of the paragraph. Throughout this section of the book, students have already read and identified openers that state main ideas.

To help students realize that they already know a lot about stating main ideas, you may review the following with them:

- The headlines they chose in Ideas for Building Background (page 39)
- The main idea sentence they stated for the Read-Aloud paragraph
- The sentences they made up for the Brainstorm activity on page 42

Have students look back at the example paragraphs in the reproducibles on pages 57–60. Explain that the first sentence in each paragraph is a topic sentence, or a sentence that states the main idea; and that the topic sentence lets the reader know what big idea the writer is going to develop.

On the chalkboard or via overhead projector, present a couple of paragraphs in which the topic sentence is missing. Have the class read the paragraph aloud, discuss what idea it seems to be developing, then compose a topic sentence. In the paragraphs that follow, possible topic sentences are shown in parentheses.

(Our Reading Circle is studying books in which the main characters have to live alone in the wilderness.) The first book our Reading Circle studied was *Julie of the Wolves,* in which the heroine learns how to survive by herself in the Arctic tundra with the help of a wolf pack. After that, we met Sam, the hero of *My Side of the Mountain*, who chose to spend a whole winter alone in the Catskill Mountains. Our Reading Circle also included Mafatu, of *Call It Courage*, in our study of wilderness heroes and heroines, even though Mafatu's wilderness was the Pacific Ocean. Now we're reading *Island of the Blue Dolphins*, in which Karana manages to survive for years on a deserted island.

(Medieval lords had to consider several things when they wanted to build a castle.) The first thing the medieval lord had to decide on was a location for the castle that could be defended in war. Hilltop locations were best for this purpose.

But the lord also had to think about peacetime and everyday life, too. The castle would be home for his family and servants, so it had to be built in a place where food supplies were ample. The lord also had to think about his duties as the ruler of a certain area of land. Could he walk or ride from his castle to different parts of his land within a day or two? Finally, the lord had to make sure that his castle was near plentiful supplies of drinking water.

COMPOSITION SKILL: HOOKING THE AUDIENCE'S INTEREST

To capture audience interest and make the audience want to read on, many writers put a "hook" sentence at the beginning of the paragraph.

1. Show Some Examples
Introduce hooks by writing the follow examples on the chalkboard and discussing them with students:

1. Sometimes the topic sentence can be phrased as a hook.
   Examples:
Here he comes, World!— our local golf champion!
That basketball game you're watching began with a peach basket in Springfeld, Massachusetts.

2. Sometimes the hook comes before the topic sentence.
   Examples:
(Hook:) Was it the crash of a giant meteor or the relentless movement of ice? (Topic sentence:) Scientists have different theories about why dinosaurs became extinct.
(Hook:) In the twilight, they come on leathery wings and begin to eat. (Topic sentence:) They are tiny bats, who free our yard of insect pests.

2. Have Students Write Hooks
Invite students to reword the following sentences to make them "hook the audience."

1. Dolphins and sea otters have ocean habitats that are much alike.
   (Example: Dolphins and sea otters are neighbors in the deep blue sea.)
2. There are many ways to have fun during a long car trip.
   (Example: When you're bored on the road, try some of these great car games!)
3. During our field trip, we found out how immigrants from many lands have built our city.
   (Example: As we traveled around our city, we found Ireland, Cuba, Germany, Nigeria, China, and Poland.)
4. An agate is a smooth, precious stone that has many colors in it.
   (Example: It's only a stone, but it sits smoothly in your hand, as if you'd caught a tiny rainbow.)

3. Use Hook Hints

Use bumper stickers, words on T-shirts, and slogans on buttons as examples of audience hooks. Present some examples, invite students to bring in their own, and then ask them to shape the words on these items into hooks for paragraphs.

WRITING PROCESS: AN EXPOSITORY PARAGRAPH

An exemplary end-product here will be an expository paragraph that states a main idea in a topic sentence and that develops the main idea through one of these strategies:

- examples
- comparison and contrast
- cause and effect
- definition and explanation
- supports the main idea with at least three well-formed sentences.

So that students can concentrate on these aspects of the paragraph, we suggest that you encourage them to start with subjects they already know a lot about. That is, students should choose subjects that don't require a lot of research. (The next section of this book deals with obtaining and using facts gleaned from research.)

▶ PREWRITING

1. Have students form four-member focus groups based on common interests. Examples:

- special holiday or cultural event
- recent field trip
- school sport or athletic event
- news event the class has discussed
- class science project
- environmental concern
- visit from a community-resource speaker or guest

2. On an overhead projector, show the class Our Group-Plans Paragraphs (page 62). Briefly discuss what the model group does:

- Selects and write the subject.
- Shows four different ways to develop the subject.
- Shows which way each group member will choose.

Then distribute copies of page 63 to each focus group. Ask group members to follow the discussion model to complete the form for their group. Be sure to circulate among the groups to help answer questions, make suggestions when kids are stuck for ideas, and offer start-up prompts for individual assignments.

3. Ask each student to write a purpose statement based on the assignment they have from their group. Review the concept that a purpose statement is for the writer alone, used to keep her or him centered on the main idea to be developed. Provide examples:

- My purpose is to give examples of after-school activities.
- My purpose is to show how after-school programs affect kids.

▶ DRAFTING

1. List Supporting Facts

Ask each student to list, in phrase or sentence form, at least three facts or ideas that are related to the purpose. Remind students that they can always consult with you or with a member of their prewriting group.

MY PURPOSE IS TO SHOW HOW AFTER-SCHOOL PROGRAMS AFFECT KIDS.

1. You feel like you have a support group to keep you from feeling lonely after school.

2. You feel safe

3. It's relaxing. There are no assignments!

4. You develop new interests, like in art or music.

MY PURPOSE IS TO DEFINE AND GIVE EXAMPLES OF AN IDEAL AFTER-SCHOOL PROGRAM.

1. It should be a place for kids with different interests: sports, music, food, putting on plays, getting homework done.
2. There are really cool adult supervisors who help you out with stuff, without stifling you.
3. It's open from 3 p.m. to 8 p.m.
4. It could be a quiet place where you could just talk with your friends.

2. Draft a Beginning

Ask students to draft a topic sentence: a sentence that states the main idea of their paragraph. Remind students that the topic sentence should be a hook that captures the audience's interest, or should be preceded by a hook sentence. Examples:

- (Topic sentence as hook): After school, there's a program that keeps me and my friends involved in what we like best.
- (Hook before topic sentence): You want art, music, dance, dramatics, and a sweaty game of volleyball? After school, there's a program that offers a lot of different activities.

3. Put It All Together

In this final step of the draft, students write their opening sentence or sentences, then shape their notes from Step 1 (List Supporting Facts) into supporting sentences to follow the opener.

► CONFERENCING

Ask the prewriting groups to come together again to discuss members' drafts. On the chalkboard or on poster paper, copy the following guidelines for groups to use as they discuss the drafts.

An Expository Paragraph

	Yes	No	Suggestions
1. The main idea is stated in a topic sentence near the beginning.			
2. The first or second sentence hooks the audience's attention.			
3. The writer focuses on one way of developing the topic: examples, or comparison and contrast, or cause and effect, or definition and example.			
4. There are at least three sentences that support the main idea with different facts.			
5. All the sentences in the paragraph relate to the main idea.			

► REVISING

Ask students to use these questions as they revise their paragraphs:

1. Which comments from your group do you find most useful? How will you use them as you revise your paragraph?
2. What new ideas of your own did you get as your group discussed your paragraph? How will you use your new ideas to improve your paragraph?
3. Think up a headline or title for your revised paragraph. The headline or title should hint at the main idea and also capture your audience's attention.

As they revise, many student writers may enjoy the challenge of incorporating connective words and phrases into their paragraphs. Connectives help relate ideas and show how they flow together. Students who have completed pages 57–60 are already familiar with these connectives, which—for students' reference—are listed at the top of those pages.

▶ PROOFREADING

1. Review the various ways writers can check spelling and ask students to use one or more of them:

- spell-checks on word processors
- dictionaries
- savvy classmate spellers
- the teacher

2. Have students work with you, with a proofreading partner, or with members of their writing group to catch and correct mechanical or grammatical errors.

▶ PUBLISHING OPTIONS

1. Ask focus groups to make a booklet of the four paragraphs group members have written. A title for the booklet might be Four Ways of Looking at...(After-School Progams) (Dolphins) (Sports Stars) (Holidays), etc. Groups can appoint members to provide illustrations, make front and back covers, and design a table of contents. Groups can put their booklets in the Reference section of your classroom library for classmates to use when they need ideas for oral or written reports.

2. Invite students to read their paragraphs aloud to the class. Specify the audience's listening tasks: What is the main idea of the paragraph? What facts support the main idea? What else would you like to know? (Suggest that the writer make notes of classmates' answers to this last question; the writer may be able to use classmates' queries in writing a longer report.)

3. For families at home and for younger students in your school, your writers can use activity 2, above. Then students can discuss in class the differences in these audiences' responses and how writers might reword their paragraphs for different audiences. This is a valuable metacognition activity, because it requires the writer to look at her or his own writing from another point of view.

4. As another metacognition strategy, invite students to discuss what was easiest and what was most difficult about writing their expository paragraphs. Deciding on a subject? Choosing a way to develop it? Framing the opening sentences? Mustering supporting facts? Encourage students to tell about their writing problems and to share ways they solved them.

ACROSS THE CURRICULUM

1. Social Studies: Famous People

In this activity, student partners summarize what they know about the accomplishments of a historical figure, then compose a brief, one-paragraph dramatic monologue for the character to speak to the class. The character can do one the following:

- Give examples of her or his accomplishments.
- Compare and contrast him or herself with another famous person.
- Show how his or her accomplishment caused a change in the lives of other people.
- Define and explain the accomplishment.

Introduce the project.

Present the project description above and add that a dramatic monologue is spoken in the first person (using *I, me, my, mine*). Explain that the dramatic monologue should be vivid and explicit enough for classmates to determine who the speaker is without being told.

Brainstorm a list of historical figures that students have recently studied.

The list may include commonly acknowledged heroes and heroines such as Harriet Tubman, Thomas Jefferson, Cesar Chavez, Amelia Earhart, Sojourner Truth, and George Washington Carver, as well as quasi-legendary figures such as John Henry, Jean Lafitte, Calamity Jane, and Daniel Boone.

Ask partners to choose a historical figure and draft a paragraph that the person might speak, without revealing her or his name.

You may wish to provide a spoken example:

> President Jefferson had given the explorers Lewis and Clark a tremendous assignment: find a Northwest passage from the East to the Pacific Ocean. These explorers could not have accomplished their exploration without me. Young as I was, and pregnant with my first baby, I managed to guide the explorers through the waterways of the American West and to help them make friends with the native peoples we met along the way. Because of my knowledge and guidance, the explorers were able to make accurate maps and gather valuable information.

After students have identified the speaker (Sacajawea) and the specific clues that helped them identify her, ask them to tell the method of development in the paragraph. (Cause and effect: how Sacajawea's knowledge and cooperation affected the work of the explorers.)

Ask partners to conference about their draft and to read it aloud.

You may wish to act as a mentor in this step. As the "try-out" audience, you can note strong points, tell which sentences or phrases do or don't present facts precisely, and talk about the method of development (e.g., examples, comparison and contrast) that partners are aiming for.

After partners have revised and proofread their paragraphs, ask them to publish orally.

They can read the paragraph aloud to the class and ask for immediate audience feedback. (Who is the historical figure? What are the clue-facts? How is the paragraph developed?) Or partners can record their paragraphs for a Speaking History Tape, which small groups of classmates can listen to so as to answer the same questions.

Other Publishing Options:

1. A dramatic-monologue presentation for families or for students in other class-rooms
2. A written anthology of the monologues, to place in the history section of your classroom bookshelf

2. Literature: Book-Briefs

A book-brief is a one-paragraph book report that concentrates on one expository strategy to tell about a major aspect of the story. Here are some suggestions to present to your students, based on the tried-and-true *Charlotte's Web*:

Use Examples. Focus on caring: Give examples of how Charlotte and Fern take care of Wilbur. Or focus on danger: Give examples of events in the story that make the reader anxious about what will happen next.

Compare and Contrast. Compare/contrast Charlotte with animal heroes and heroines in other books. How is Charlotte like the wolves in *Julie of the Wolves*? How is she different from the befuddled Pooh in Winnie-the-Pooh?

Cause-and-Effect. How does Wilbur's plight affect other animals in the barn? Or, how does Charlotte's kindness and wisdom change the other animals' behavior and attitudes toward life and death?

Define/Explain. Define friendship. Then, using your definition, explain why Charlotte is a true friend to Wilbur.

Some students may wish to work independently to choose a book and write a brief. Or students who've chosen the same book may wish to work together in a focus group, with each of the members concentrating on a different expository strategy. In either case, remind students that their paragraphs should begin with a sentence that hooks the audience. Suggest some publishing options:

- Place your Book Brief in a Reviewers' Folder next to the book on the classroom library shelf. After a classmate has read the book and your Brief, discuss points of agreement and disagreement.
- Post your Book Brief under a **Read This!** banner on a bulletin board.
- Read your Book Brief aloud to the class.
- If you've written Book Briefs with a group, use them to make a longer book report.

WORKPLACE SKILL:
WRITING A LETTER OF INQUIRY

Your students may often have questions they wish to ask of manufacturers, government figures, book authors, officials of organizations, and of other people they don't know personally. The following activity will help students apply their expository writing skills to composing the body of such letters. (Since these are business letters, you may want to follow-up by teaching or reviewing the business-letter form, using any standard grammar-and-composition textbook.)

On an overhead, show a good model of a letter of inquiry. Lead students in a discussion of (1) how the first sentence presents the main idea, (2) how all the other sentences relate to the main idea, (3) the brevity of the letter, and (4) how all these factors add up to a letter that catches the recipient's attention.

10799 Sixth Avenue
Petunia, Arkansas (ZIP)
May 8, 1998

Birds-Are-Us
11 Mountain Street
Flatland, Maine (ZIP)

Dear People at Birds-Are-Us:

I've designed and built a bird-feeder that squirrels can't get to and that bluejays can't tip over and spill! The feeder is built of inexpensive materials and can be put together pretty easily. I think people who feed birds all year round would like to have an invention like mine.
If you would like to see my design, please let me know.

Sincerely,
Tina Brandt

Next, show a letter of inquiry that needs editing. (1)Discuss the ways the letter "wanders." (2) Ask students to find the topic sentence (sentence #3), reword it, and place it at the beginning. (3) Have students identify the sentences that don't relate to the main idea (sentences #2 and #6). (4) Ask students to compose one or two other sentences that do relate to the main idea. (5) Write students' edited versions on the chalkboard.

12 Cook Street
Pietop, Montana (ZIP)
April 1, 1998

Yum Foods Corporation
River Forest Road
Smithers, Minnesota (ZIP)

Dear Yum Foods:

  I think there are a couple of steps missing. Almost everyone likes a few snacks after school. On your package of Flitter Bits, the directions aren't clear. What do you do after crunching up the jelly beans? Does "cook" mean boil or roast?
  Flitter Bits might make a good party food.

Sincerely,
Eduardo Esposito

Invite students to write expository paragraphs for letters of inquiry. Examples:
- Ask a local SPCA about summer or weekend jobs at the animal shelter.
- Ask a favorite author if she or he would visit your classroom and tell why you would appreciate such a visit.
- Tell a manufacturer of weed-killers about specific concerns and questions you have about their product.
- Ask a local or national political figure for his or her position on an issue that matters to you.
- Tell a TV executive about the kinds of programs you like and ask why there are not more of these programs.
- Write a Web inquiry asking for information on a specific assignment you have in school.

Encourage publishing. For some students, this may simply involve conferencing and revising with a partner, then sharing the final paragraph with a group of classmates. Other students may wish in addition to implement business-letter form, send their letters, and share any responses with the class.

TEST-TAKING SKILL: THINKING LIKE A WRITER

Many items on standardized tests call on students to use their ability to provide examples, compare and contrast, link cause and effect, define or explain, or grasp a main idea. All these skills relate to the concepts about expository writing that your students have been practicing. To help students apply these skills to test questions, use the following items. Explain what writing-and-thinking skill the test-taker will use. After students have decided on the answer, explain, or have a student explain, why the correct answer is correct and why the three other options aren't.

Test Questions
(Some questions ask you to give examples.)

Circle the letter of the correct answer.

1. Which one is an example of a bird?   (a)

(a) robin   (b) deer   (c) puppy   (d) lizard

2. Which one is not an example of a shelter?   (d)

(a) tent   (b) house   (c) cave   (d) sandwich

(Some questions ask you to compare or contrast.)

3. Night is to **Day** as **Good** is to: (b)

(a) pretty   (b) bad   (c) light   (d) correct

4. High is to **Up** as **Low** is to: (c)

(a) over   (b) inside   (c) down   (d) around

(Some questions expect you to see cause and effect.)

5. Happiness brings **laughter** just as **sadness** brings   (d)

(a) words   (b) letters   (c) rain   (d) tears

6. After a blizzard, you expect to see: (a)

(a) snow banks   (b) flowers   (c) skateboarders   (d) fires

(Some questions ask you to define or explain something.)

7. Which one is not part of a forest? (c)
(a) an undergrowth of shrubs and bushes
(b) a canopy of tall trees
(c) coral reefs and and sand dunes
(d) a variety of plants and animals

8. Which one tells about stages of growth? (b)
(a) hands, mittens, gloves
(b) infant, teenager, adult
(c) ponds, lakes, rivers
(d) sailboat, submarine, canoe

(Some questions require you to find the main idea.)

9. Read the paragraph. Write the letter of the best title. (a)
A snorkel is an easy device for breathing while your head is underwater. The snorkle tube extends above the water. You hold the mouthpiece tightly between your lips and breathe air in and out through your mouth as you swim just below the surface.
(a) How to Use a Snorkel
(b) Sea Life in the Ocean
(c) Conquering Fear of Water
(d) Ways to Survive in the Sea

10. Which idea does not belong in a report about the history of flight? (d)
(a) early attempts at manned flight
(b) the Wright brothers' first planes
(c) the development of rockets
(d) my first trip on a plane

Name _____

DEVELOPING A MAIN IDEA THROUGH EXAMPLES

Some words and phrases that focus on **EXAMPLES:**

for example	**as an example**	**another way**	**another kind**
for instance	**also, and**	**in addition**	

1. Read the paragraph. Underline the words and phrases that focus on examples.

Even if you live in a big city, you can be a nature sleuth. For example, you can observe and make notes about different kinds of birds that hang out in parks or even on sidewalks and window ledges. Also, you can draw sketches of different kinds of wild plants that seem to survive in a city environment. For instance, young plane trees, dandelions, and different varieties of grass may spring up in pavement cracks, in vacant lots, and along railroad tracks.

2. Check the title that best fits the paragraph above.

_____ Why Birds Like a City Environment

_____ Looking for Wildlife in the City

_____ Things to Do in a Big City

3. Write two or three sentences of your own to add to the paragraph above.
In each of your sentences, use a word or phrase from the list at the top of this page.

_____

_____

_____

_____

_____

_____

Name _____

DEVELOPING A MAIN IDEA THROUGH COMPARISON AND CONTRAST

Some words and phrases that focus on **COMPARISON AND CONTRAST:**

alike	**similar**	**have in common**	**both**	**same**
in the same way	**different**	**differences**	**unlike**	**also**
on the other hand	**however**	**instead**	**but**	

1. Read the paragraph. Then check the phrase below it that tells the writer's purpose.

> Thanksgiving and the Fourth of July come at different times of the year, but both holidays are important to me. These holidays are alike for me because they're times for my family and friends to gather together. Also, both holidays are full of special decorations and foods. On the other hand, these two holidays are different in some ways. Unlike our Thanksgiving meal, our Fourth of July feast is held outdoors. After Thanksgiving dinner, the family tends to take naps or watch TV; however, after our Fourth of July picnic, we all want to stay awake and watch the fireworks.

The writer's purpose is to:

_____ tell how two holidays are the same and different.

_____ explain why one holiday is more important than the other.

_____ describe a Fourth of July celebration.

2. In the paragraph above, underline the words and phrases that helped you understand the writer's purpose.

3. Choose two holidays you like. Use the Venn diagram to compare and contrast them.

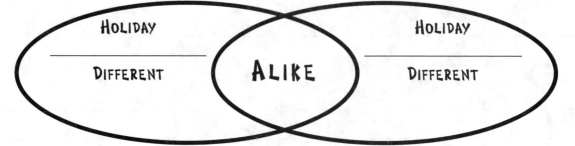

DEVELOPING A MAIN IDEA THROUGH CAUSE AND EFFECT

Some words and phrases that focus on **CAUSE AND EFFECT:**

so	because	leads/led to	for this reason	as a result
then	if	when	caused by	due to consequently

1. Read the paragraph. Underline the words and phrases that focus on cause and effect.

> Due to mosquitoes and other stinging insects, we couldn't enjoy our yard last summer. This year, we put bat houses around the yard, and for this reason our insect problem is almost solved. Because bats eat insects, the mosquito population around our property has dwindled a lot. So we can sit comfortably outside at night, enjoying a bug-free environment—all as a result of welcoming tiny bats!

2. Underline the sentence that would fit best in the paragraph above. Be ready to support your choice.

_____ Bats appear as dangerous characters in many horror stories.

_____ If you put up bat houses, bats will be attracted to your property.

_____ Bats look like "flying mice," but they're really a different species.

3. Use the information in the paragraph above to complete these cause-and-effect sentences.

Putting up houses for bats leads to _____

_____

Our neighbors decided to put bat houses in their yards when they _____

_____

The bats are attracted to the special houses you put up for them, and then they _____

_____

_____

Name _____

DEVELOPING A MAIN IDEA THROUGH DEFINITION AND EXPLANATION

Some words and phrases that focus on **DEFINITION AND EXPLANATION:**

is/are	**began as**	**here's how**	**is/are made up of**
consist of	**for/as an example**	**means**	**described as**
same/different	**like**	**also**	**first, next, then, finally**

1. Read the paragraph. The sentences are numbered so that you can use them for the activities that follow the paragraph.

(1) A habitat is the place where a living thing usually lives and meets its needs for survival. (2) These needs are made up of food, water, air, space, and shelter. (3) For example, a bottle-nosed dolphin's habitat is the ocean. (4) There the dolphin eats fish, gets water from its food, gets air from above the water, claims coastal waters as its usual space, and finds shelter in the open ocean. (5) The ocean is also the sea otter's habitat. (6) Like dolphins, sea otters get food and water from other ocean animals, breathe air above the water, and move around in waters near the coast. (7) One difference in dolphin and otter habitat is shelter. (8) The otter's shelter consists of rocks and kelp beds.

2. Write the number of the sentence or sentences that:
_____ define the word habitat
_____ explain what the survival needs are for all living things
_____ explain and give examples of a dolphin's habitat
_____ explain and give examples of another animal's habitat

3. Underline the words and phrases in the paragraph that focus on definition and explanation. (Refer to the list at the top of the page.)

4. With a partner, choose one of the following to define and explain. Underline your choice.

latitude	a barometer	a guitar	the rainbow	Thanksgiving
continent	a journal	planet	money	the Internet

On a separate sheet of paper, draft a sentence or two that defines the subject you chose. Draft two or three sentences that begin to explain the subject.

STRATEGIES FOR DEVELOPING THE SUBJECT

Through
EXAMPLES
Describe different kinds of dinosaurs.

Through
COMPARISON AND CONTRAST
Tell how the dinosaurs' environment was different from our own today.

SUBJECT:
DINOSAURS

Through
CAUSE AND EFFECT
Tell what may have caused dinosaurs to become extinct.

Through
DEFINITION AND EXPLANATION
Define what a reptile is and explain why most dinosaurs fit into the reptile category.

OUR GROUP-PLANS PARAGRAPHS

OUR SUBJECT: After-School Programs for Kids in Our Community

GIVE EXAMPLES
What are some of the after-school activities kids can participate in?

USE COMPARISON AND CONTRAST
How are these programs alike and different from programs in other neighborhoods?

WAYS TO DEVELOP THE SUBJECT

SHOW CAUSE AND EFFECT
Why do we need after-school programs? How do they help kids?

DEFINE AND EXPLAIN
What does the ideal after-school program consist of? Why would this program be ideal?

Group Writers:

EXAMPLES: Sharon

COMPARING AND CONTRASTING: Jaime

CAUSE AND EFFECT: Tabitha

DEFINE AND EXPLAIN: Lee

OUR GROUP-PLANS PARAGRAPHS

OUR SUBJECT _____

GIVE EXAMPLES
_____
_____
_____

USE COMPARISON AND CONTRAST
_____
_____
_____

WAYS TO DEVELOP THE SUBJECT

SHOW CAUSE AND EFFECT
_____
_____
_____

DEFINE AND EXPLAIN
_____
_____
_____

Group Writers:

EXAMPLES: _____

COMPARING AND CONTRASTING: _____

CAUSE AND EFFECT: _____

DEFINE AND EXPLAIN: _____

PART FOUR

WRITING A REPORT

Review sources of information.

Plan and carry out successful interviews.

Organize notes.

Write a multi-paragraph report.

GETTING STARTED

PREPARATION

For each student, make copies of reproducible pages 83, 84, 85, and 86. For the Building Background activity, arrange a labeled display of examples of familiar resource materials—for example, general encyclopedias, special reference books such as nature and biographical encyclopedias, nonfiction trade books, news-related media such as newspapers and periodicals, Web addresses and CD-ROM disks, atlases, social studies and science textbooks, subject-specific magazines such as *Zoobooks* or *Calliope*, videotapes on real-life subjects.

IDEA FOR BUILDING BACKGROUND

Most of your students have probably had experience in previous grades with using print resource materials to get information on specific topics. You can use the following activities to check and build students' skills in this area.

Review sources of information.

On the chalkboard, write the broad subjects shown below.

sea mammals	sports heroes and heroines	exploring outer space
dinosaurs	popular movies	climbing mountains
insects	kids' problems	famous writers
disasters	endangered animals	ways to draw pictures

Ask partners to choose a subject and then to study your display of resources (see Preparation, above) to determine which ones they'd consult to find information on their subject. Partners should identify the resources and write questions they'd expect the resource to answer. Examples:

Subject: Dinosaurs

Source: General Enyclopedia
What were some kinds of dinosaurs? Where did they live? What may have led to their extinction?

Source: News (Magazines and Newspapers)
What are the latest findings and ideas about dinosaurs?

Source: Textbooks
What other kinds of life existed in the days of the dinosaurs?

Source: Videotapes
How did dinosaurs move around? What did Earth look like in the time of the dinosaurs?

Subject: Climbing Mountains

Source: Atlas
Which are the world's highest mountains? Where are they located?

Source: Nonfiction books
Who are some famous explorers who first climbed these great mountains? What challenges did they encounter? What did they say about their adventures?

Source: The Web
Who is planning to climb these mountains today? What qualifications and skills does a person need to qualify for these climbs?

Encourage partners to share their lists of resources and questions with other groups and to note other possible questions and suggest other possible sources of information.

Choose your questions.

Now flip-flop the above activity. Ask each student to write the two questions he or she would most like to answer in a report on his or her subject. Beneath the questions, have the student write at least three resources he or she can use to find answers to the questions. Examples:

MY SUBJECT: EXPLORING OTHER PLANETS

MY QUESTIONS:

Why do we want to explore other planets?

What are some things we've learned so far about other planets?

RESOURCES:

Encyclopedia	Nonfiction books about solar system
News articles	Biographies of space explorers
Science magazines	Web pages

MY SUBJECT: FAVORITE ILLUSTRATORS OF KIDS' BOOKS

MY QUESTIONS:

Who are some illustrators that kids my age like best?

How did these artists get started in their careers?

RESOURCES:

A survey of classmates' favorites

Biographical dictionaries

Autobiographies of book illustrators

LISTENING TO AN INTERVIEW

Skillful interviewing serves student writers in important ways:

- Interviews can supply original information to include in reports.
- Planning and carrying out interviews requires students to keep focusing on main ideas.
- Interviewing provides oral language practice and opportunities to listen and respond empathetically.

Introduce the Activity

Ask students to tell about memorable interviews they've heard on TV or radio. Who was the interviewer? the interviewee? What did the students learn: new information? unusual viewpoints? Make sure students understand the difference between an interview and a round-table discussion or debate. An interviewer asks questions and gives prompts that encourage the interviewee to tell about his or her activities, ideas, and memories. The interviewer does not pass judgments, argue, or make speeches. In a good interview, 90% of the words will come from the interviewee.

Review the Key Words

Write the words **who**, **what**, **when**, **where**, **why**, and **how** on the chalkboard. Explain that these are the Key Words to use in an interview, because they're the ones that will get the interviewee to supply details. Interviewers try to avoid questions that require only yes or no answers. Provide examples of questions that don't and do result in information.

- **Interviewer:** Did you have fun on the Fourth of July?
- **Interviewee:** Yes.
- **Interviewer:** Do your neighbors celebrate the same holidays?
- **Interviewee:** No.

To get information, begin your questions with the Key Words.

- **Interviewer:** How did you celebrate the Fourth of July when you were a little kid?
- **Interviewee:** We had a big family picnic, and then we all went to Green Lake and took a swim.
- **Interviewer:** What are some of the holidays your neighbors celebrate?
- **Interviewee:** Well, next door my neighbors do Kwanza. Down the street, there's a Dawali celebration once a year. For my family, there's Hannukah. Right after that, my friend Leo celebrates Christmas. Seems like we're always celebrating something around here!

Model an Interview

You play the part of the interviewer, or host. A student volunteer will be the guest, or interviewee. For the interview, choose a "safe" subject such as one of the following:

School Highlights	Favorite Holidays
Exciting Vacations	The Best Pets
Favorite Books	Adventures with Friends

Ask the student audience to listen to the interview to note the **w-h** words that your questions begin with and any helpful prompts you use to elicit more information, such as "Please tell me more about that." "That story really helps me understand better. I bet you have more stories like that!"

Keep the interview brief (five-minute maximum). Invite other students to be your interviewees. Test the waters: Some students may wish to conduct interviews with a partner. Ideally, you'll tape-record interviews so that small groups can listen to them and discuss what they liked best about the interviews and what they think might have improved them.

On the basis of a whole-class follow-up discussion, students can brainstorm a list of Hints for Interviewers.

PLANNING AND CONDUCTING AN INTERVIEW

Planning an interview requires the student writer to:

- state the main idea she or he wishes to develop in a report.
- list a few **w-h** questions that the writer hopes will be answered in an interview or interviews.
- list persons the writer might interview to get the answers.

To help students plan, distribute the reproducible Planning an Interview (page 83). Preview the prompts with the class, then ask students to work with a partner or small group to complete the page.

Bring the class together to discuss any problems they predict. Many of these may involve how to access prospective interviewees who aren't "locals." Suggest the following accesses:

- Write a letter to the interviewee. Write your questions briefly. You might design your letter as a questionnaire: Leave space under each question for the interviewee's response.
- Conduct a telephone interview.
- Search through the Internet for Web pages or addresses of prospective interviewees. Conduct your interview.

To conduct a successful interview, writers also need to follow certain before-and-after steps. Distribute the reproducible Before-and-After Interview Checklist (page 84). Preview the prompts with the class and ask students to follow them as they set up and conclude their interviews.

TAKING NOTES

So that students don't get lost in a swamp of loose notes, encourage them to choose and use one specific organizational method. Examples:

1. Use separate notebook pages for each major question you'd like your report to answer. Write the question at the top of the page. After you take notes that help to answer the question, write the source of your information.

WHAT DID KIDS DO FOR SUMMER FUN IN OUR COMMUNITY LONG AGO?

Hay-rides: going out at night in a horse-drawn wagon and singing songs along the way. (Town Historical Museum pictures and captions) Street games: hopscotch, jumprope, stickball, and hide-and-seek. "We liked to play these games after supper. Our parents would holler 'Come in! It's getting dark!' But we stayed out, because it was fun playing in the twilight." (interview with Mrs. Goldberg) Little League: "A lot of boys got involved in this. Girls weren't allowed way back then!" (interview with Mrs. Goldberg)

2. Use index cards. In capital letters, write each question on a separate index card. Note on separate index cards the answers you got from each source. Note the source. File your notes to follow the question they answer.

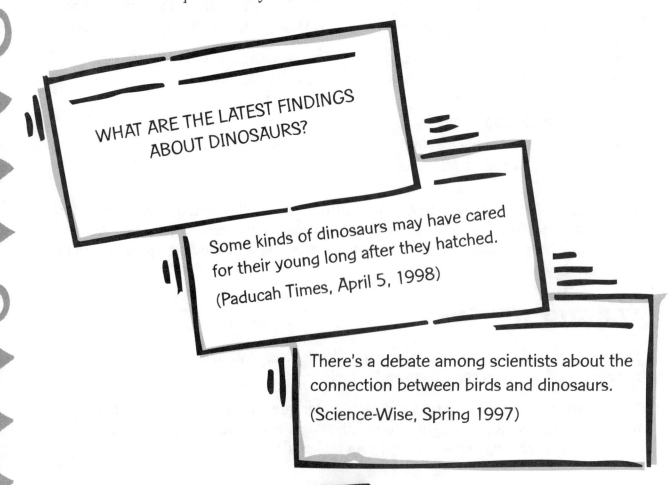

WHAT ARE THE LATEST FINDINGS ABOUT DINOSAURS?

Some kinds of dinosaurs may have cared for their young long after they hatched. (Paducah Times, April 5, 1998)

There's a debate among scientists about the connection between birds and dinosaurs. (Science-Wise, Spring 1997)

3. Create a visual organizer, such as an idea web or a chart, for each main question and the notes and sources that apply to it.

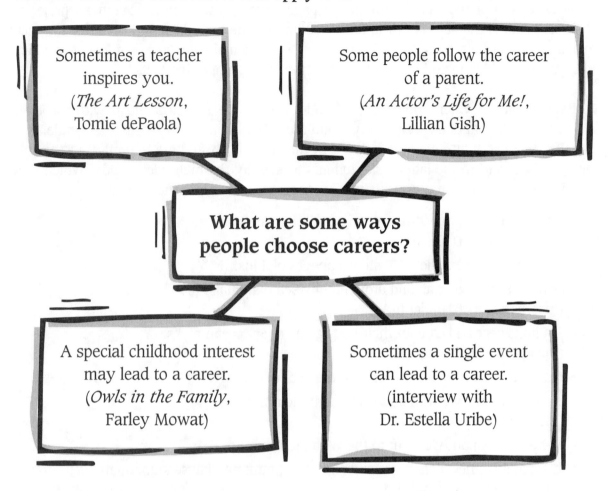

COMPOSITION SKILL: MAKING AN OUTLINE

For the expository writer, outlining is a prewriting strategy for organizing major ideas and the facts that support them. If your students have been using any of the note-taking strategies suggested on pages 69–70, they are already well-launched in outlining: Their note pages, file cards, charts, or idea webs organize ideas and supporting data in graphic ways.

A few superstar, experienced writers may be able to construct good reports just by using these notes. However, most young writers benefit from making a more formal outline. Constructing one helps the student not only organize data but also to identify and discard irrelevant facts and to note main ideas for which more supporting data is needed.

We suggest that you help students practice the traditional outline format for organizing two-or three-paragraph reports.

1. Make copies of the sample outline on page 85 or show it on an overhead projector. Discuss: What is the subject of the report? What are the main ideas? (I, II, III) What facts explain or support each main idea? (A's, B's, C's) Each main idea needs at least three facts to support it. Which main idea needs at least two more supporting facts?

2. Explain that a writer's notes may include facts or ideas that do fit in with the main ideas, and facts that don't. List or say aloud the following facts and ideas. Ask students to identify the ones that have little to do with the subject (N) and are important to the subject (Y). In regard to the latter, ask students to identify the main ideas under which they belong, and write, or have students write, correct responses into the outline.

- Most mammals protect their young until they are mature. (Y)
  (Incorporate as D, under I.)
- There are some excellent TV shows about dolphins. (N)
- Fishers' seine nets trap and drown many sea mammals. (Y)
  (Incorporate as B, under III.)
- Sea lions bear and care for their young on craggy ocean rocks. (Y)
  (Incorporate as D, under II.)
- We went to a show at SeaWorld and fed some seals. (N)
- Baby whales travel with and learn from their mothers. (Y)
  (Incorporate as E, under II.)
- At Mystic Seaport, we went to the Whaling Museum. (N)
- In some countries, fishers are still allowed to hunt and kill sea mammals. (Y)
  (Incorporate as C, under III.)

3. Distribute copies of An Outline of My Report (page 86). Preview the activity with the class, then ask students to work independently, with a student partner or, with you to make an outline for their report.

PUTTING IDEAS TOGETHER

As students begin to draft expository paragraphs, we often instruct them to "tell where you got your information" and also to "state your ideas in your own way." These are tall orders! Most student writers need to study examples and then practice these strategies before they can successfully use them in their reports. You may use the following activities. To aid discussion, duplicate the examples for distribution or prepare them for use on an overhead projector.

ACTIVITIES

1. Quoting Sources

Example for discussion

My Subject: **A City Summer Long Ago**

Source:

Grandpa Laskowski's words on an interview tape:

I used to play kick-the-can with Eddie O'Brian and the Sanchez kids. We liked to play at night, under the stars and street lights, while neighbors sat on stoops and cheered us on.

Writer's Report Sentence:

Mr. Laskowski remembers playing kick-the-can with his friends. "We liked to play at night, under the stars and streetlights, while neighbors sat on stoops and cheered us on," he said.
(**Quote all of a sentence.**)

Source:

A Parks Department booklet from the year 1939:

City pools and beaches are open to all residents and their guests, but will be closed whenever incidents of polio would threaten public health.

Writer's Report Sentence:

There were plenty of places to swim, but they were shut down when "incidents of polio would threaten public health."
(**Quote part of a sentence.**)

Point out that writers usually directly quote only statements that are particularly colorful ("We liked to play...[etc.]") or particularly concise ("incidents of...[etc.]").

Next, have students work in small groups to brainstorm ways to quote whole sentences, then parts of sentences, from a taped interview with Mr. Zee, a neighbor, for a report on the subject of Summer Fun.

Mr. Zee: I got a reputation as the Water Guy, because I was the only one who dared to turn on the hydrants so that we could all splash around, just like happy fish in a cool pond. That was 50 years ago. I guess savvy kids today don't turn on hydrants anymore. Maybe it's because the fire department cracks down on them, or because they know there's a water shortage. Keeping cool is what it's always been about, though! You kids today go down to the City Rec Pool. When I was a kid, we didn't have a ready-made lake like that.

Invite students to use written resources or their taped interviews to write sentences in which they directly quote all or part of the information. With partners, students can discuss why they think the material is particularly worthy of being quoted word-for-word.

You may wish to do a spot check to determine which students need to review the mechanics of writing direct quotations, then group these students for instruction.

2. Reword Information to Say It Your Way

An expository report should reflect the writer's special way of presenting ideas. Unless a source's exact words are especially colorful or precise, the writer should restate facts in her or his own way.

Example for discussion

My Subject: **A City Summer Long Ago**

From interview tape with Mrs. Frank:	**Rewording for my report:**
Well, I don't know exactly...we used to have some kind of bike contests, sort a rodeo. Like, we found an empty lot or something, and we set up obstacles... maybe barrels or big cartons, and we had to go around them, you know, real fast, if you wanted to win.	How about a Bike Rodeo? Mrs. Frank said that kids used to set up barrels and cartons in an empty lot. Then they'd get on their bikes and race around the obstacles. **(Clarify the information.)**
From County Museum booklet:	**Rewording for my report:**
The development of the electric trolley car in the early years of the twentieth century enabled many families to travel out of town for a day's outing or picnic in the countryside.	In the early 1900s, electric trolley cars came to our area. Families used them to make picnic trips to the country. **(Restate the information in your own way.)**

Ask students to reword any of their interviewees' responses that need clarification and tightening up. Have students work with partners to compare the original with the rewrite. Is the rewrite clearer? Does it convey the original idea accurately? Does the rewrite sound natural, like the writer's own unique way (style) of saying things? How could the rewrite be improved?

REVIEW YOUR AUDIENCE'S NEEDS

The writer thinks about the audience by considering these questions:

- What does my audience already know about my subject?
- What new facts or ideas can I supply that will interest my audience and add to their knowledge about the subject?
- What kind of language (sentence structure, vocabulary, order of ideas) should I use to keep my audience tracking along with me?

You may wish to use the following activities with students who need additional practice in shaping their writing for specific audiences.

ACTIVITIES

1. Write for Your Classmates: Supply New Information

Have students form Expert Groups, six to eight students per group. The group chooses a subject that they and their classmates are familiar with, such as a favorite sport, a holiday they've all explored, or a recently completed science or social studies investigation. Then:

- Together, group members brainstorm a list of key facts they all know about the chosen subject. Then the group drafts a paragraph (starting with a topic sentence) that incorporates three or four of the major facts.
- The group divides into two teams. Each team is responsible for finding, through research, at least two interesting facts that relate to the topic but that are NOT in the group list or paragraph.
- Each team then writes a revised draft of the group paragraph, incorporating the "new" facts the team has discovered.
- Teams share and discuss their paragraphs. What's new in the paragraph? Is the information interesting? How does it relate to the main idea?
- The group works together to write a final draft that incorporates the best suggestions from both teams.
- A group spokesperson reads the final paragraph to the class. The audience listens to determine: What does the paragraph say that I already knew? What does it say that is new to me; that is, what did I learn?

2. Make Audience Profiles

Show the following graphic on an overhead projector. Discuss what it tells about the two ways to approach a subject, depending on who the writer's audience is.

SUBJECT: OUR MASKED BALL

Audience: **Little kids**

Audience: **Families at Home**

What They Already Know

- The second-grade has seen us making masks and heard us playing music in the gym.

- They know that masks are fun, and that music is fun, too.

- They've received our invitations to a Musical History Masked Ball.

- They know we're studying American History.

- They know a "ball" can mean a series of dances.

What They Would Like To Know

- What is our class getting ready for?

- What's a "masked ball"? Do you put a mask on a soccer ball?

- Is it a party? Can our second grade come to it?

- What has music got to do with American History?

- Are guests going to have to dance and make masks?

- What are you and your class learning from this project?

Discuss with the class how knowing their audience will affect what they say in a paragraph on a specific subject. Will a paragraph for little kids say the same thing as a paragraph for adults? Why or why not? Invite volunteers to state the subject they plan to write about and then give examples of different topic sentences or hooks they might use for different audiences.

WRITING PROCESS: A REPORT

An exemplary end-product will be a report that:

- sticks to a specific subject.
- uses a specific strategy (e.g., cause-and-effect or examples).
- begins with a topic sentence about the subject.
- consists of at least two paragraphs about the subject, each paragraph developing a main idea.
- shows that the writer has used at least three different sources in gathering data for the report.

▶ PREWRITING

1. Describe the task to students by presenting the criteria above and listing them on the chalkboard.

2. To reassure students that they already have all or most of the tools for fulfilling the criteria, ask them to get together the following:

- their subject statements and lists of questions (page 66)
- their notes from interviews and other sources
- their outlines

3. You may wish to have students work with you or a partner to determine whether they need to fill in any gaps in their start-up materials (**2**, above). In their notes, have they noted the sources of their information? Are their outlines complete, with at least three supporting facts for each main idea? Have they written a writer's purpose statement and/or a start-up topic sentence? Have they decided on the expository strategy they'll use in their reports?

You may allot one class period to the prewriting tasks. Suggest that students who already have these tasks well in hand help classmates who need a partner's input or suggestions at this stage.

▶ DRAFTING

Most students will need at least two class periods for writing drafts.

1. Start with a Just-Write
Remind students that at this stage, they're not writing a final report but instead are using their materials to "rehearse" their ideas on paper.

To emphasize the rehearsal nature of the first draft, ask students to use pencil and to write on every-other line of their paper. If students are using word processors to draft, they should triple-space and use an identifying label, e.g., First Draft: report on neighborhood holidays.

2. Continue with a Free-Read

The free-read process is probably the most valuable critical tool a writer can employ. In listening to his or her words said aloud, without comment from an audience, the writer discovers more about the strengths and weaknesses of a piece of writing than through using any other strategy. Some free-read methods:

- "Whisper-read" your draft to yourself.
- Read your draft to a partner or to a small group of classmates.
- Tape-record your reading of your first draft, then listen to your tape.
- Read your draft to your teacher.

Immediately after the free-read, the student writes his or her own corrections, additions, or comments on the draft. Suggest that the writer refer to the criteria you've listed (see Prewriting).

3. Write a Second Draft

Ask students to write a new draft of their reports, using the ideas and corrections they've made as a result of their free-reads. Advise students to label their second drafts and to keep the first draft for possible reference later on.

▶ CONFERENCING

Ask students to work with a writing partner to discuss their second drafts. You may wish to distribute copies of the Checklist on page 87 for partners to use as a discussion guide. You can also adapt the Checklist to serve as an assessment tool when you're reading students' final reports.

▶ REVISING AND PROOFREADING
1. Make a Third Draft

Ask students to use their partners' comments and their own free-read ideas to make a third and final draft of their reports.

2. Correct Mechanical and Spelling Errors

With you or with a classmate writing partner, students check to make sure that:

- each paragraph is indented.
- words are spelled correctly.
- punctuation marks are used correctly around quoted phrases or sentences.
- capital letters are used where they belong for example, to begin sentences to begin proper names of people and places and to begin the important words in titles of books you're quoting from.

3. Write a Snappy Title for Your Report

Explore with students how good titles, like good hook sentences, can get immediate attention from the writer's audience. Students may review the headlines on page 40 for ideas.

Some students may wish to incorporate visuals, unusual lettering, illuminated capitals, or border designs into the openings of their reports.

► PUBLISHING OPTIONS

1. Look over students' reports to determine some general categories they fall under, for example, Science, History, Holidays, Sports, Animals, Books. Make a labeled folder for each category and place the folders on a reading table. For each folder entry, include a Reader's Comments page like the one shown below.

Then ask each student to read aloud to the class the title and first paragraph of his or her report. Have the writer and the class determine which folder the report belongs in.

History Reports
READER'S COMMENTS

2. Have students work in groups of five or six to continue the writers' metacognition discussion that they began when discussing paragraphs (page 50). Possible questions for discussion: What were the easiest steps in writing my report? What were some difficult problems I ran into, and how did I solve them? If I were going to write a report on the same subject again, what would I do differently? What important things did I learn about writing?

ACROSS THE CURRICULUM

Critical Reading:
Critiquing a Report in a Periodical
To encourage them in their own writing, students need to know that even professional writers seldom produce "perfect" products. Reassemble the periodicals you used for Building Background, page 65. Have partners choose one of the articles, read it in its entirety, and then critique it using the following criteria:

- Do the headline and opening sentences tell me exactly what the article is about? Would we change them if we could? How?

- What's the main idea of the article? Has the writer stuck to the main idea?

- Does each paragraph develop an idea by using several supporting facts?

- What questions do I have about this subject that the article doesn't answer?

Study Skills: Noting Main Ideas in a Textbook

Most textbooks provide clues to main ideas and details that students can use before they start to read a section or chapter from start to finish. By using these clues, students will find their study tasks easier. With your class's science or social studies textbook, point out these examples:

- At the end of each section, there are usually some questions or problems to respond to. Read these questions or problems first, before you begin the section, because they're clues to the main facts you should look for as you read.
- At the beginning of a textbook section, there is often a highlighted paragraph that you should read carefully, because it's a clue to the main idea of the section.
- Before you read, scan the boldfaced headings in the section. These are clues to the supporting ideas that will be developed.
- Before you read, study pictures and other graphics and any captions that go with them. These are also clues to the main stuff you should look for as you read.

To show students that these study skills actually work, select a textbook section that the class hasn't studied yet, have students move through the steps above, ask them to read the section in its entirety, then ask them to respond to the questions that end the section. Encourage feed-back: How do skimming and scanning for main ideas make studying easier?

Literature: Writing a Report About Two Books

Ask students to choose two favorite books and to write a report that compares and contrasts the main characters in them. Suggest this procedure:

- **First paragraph:** Begin with a topic sentence and a hook that gets the audience interested in your books. Continue with at least three sentences that tell briefly why both main characters are interesting.
- **Second paragraph:** Focus on the main character in one of your books. Write three or four sentences that summarize what the character does and discovers as the story moves along.
- **Third paragraph:** Focus on the main character in the second book you've chosen. For this character, too, tell what he or she does or discovers.
- **Fourth paragraph:** Write three or four sentences that tell how the two characters are alike and different.

You may wish to provide a model:

TWO ADVENTURERS

What's it like to live all alone? I've never tried it myself, but there are two book characters who have helped me understand the challenges. In **THE TALKING EARTH**, Billie Wind goes through the Florida Everglades by herself to test her people's belief that all living things have much to teach human beings. In **CALL IT COURAGE**, Mafatu must sail off by himself to overcome his fear of the ocean.

Billie Wind starts her journey with a lot of doubts. Can she really find parts of the Earth that talk to her? Her questions are soon answered when she has to hide from a forest fire and when she observes animals and plants to figure out how to survive in the Everglades.

Mafatu undertakes his ocean trip alone because he must prove to his kinfolk that he is worthy to be part of a seafaring people. Among the dangers he encounters are wild storms, vicious sharks, and being washed up on an desert island. Mafatu discovers that he can use his wits to survive, and he goes back home feeling victorious.

Billie Wind and Mafatu are different in important ways. For example, Billie Wind starts her adventure feeling brave, whereas Mafatu starts his trip feeling frightened. Billie Wind wants to test traditional beliefs, whereas Mafatu wants to test himself. These two characters are alike in an important way, however. They both discover their personal strengths and find out much about the natural world in which they live.

WORKPLACE SKILL: TEACHING OTHERS

Explain to students that in many jobs and careers, experienced workers must teach new employees how to carry out specific tasks. Segue into a discussion of the following ideas:

- Most of us have strong points, or subjects and skills that we know a lot about. Call on students to list strong skills of their classmates. Examples:
  - Lita is an expert soccer player.
  - Bernard illustrates stories really well.
  - Gavin is great at finding the main idea in an article.
  - Renee seems to know all about computers.
  - Phil is real good at solving disputes.

Most of us have weak points, or subjects and skills we'd like to know more about. Ask volunteers to use the list above to identify classmates who might help them build a desired skill or understand a particular subject.

Ask students to organize themselves into groups according to the skill or subject they will focus on. Each group will consist of a teacher, or "expert," and four or five learners, or "new employees."

Present the responsibilities of learners and teachers:

Learners:
State what it is that you wish to learn. Examples:

- I want to learn how to move paragraphs around on a word processor.
- I want to learn how to make a good outline for a report.

Always ask questions or ask for more help when you don't understand something. Examples:

- Tell me again how to use the keys to move a paragraph.
- How do I turn an outline entry into a good sentence?

Teachers:
Find out what your "learners" wish to learn.

Give your instructions in clear ways. You can use one or more of the following strategies:

- Show and explain the process step by step.
- Use examples.
- Compare and contrast the skill with other skills.
- Demonstrate cause and effect. How does one step affect the next one?
- Test your teaching skills: Have your learners carry out the procedure. If your instructions are great and your audience has been paying attention, all your students will show that they can be superstars.

In addition to its value as an application of expository strategies, this Workplace Skill activity allows each student to be both a teacher and a learner. For example, a student who is a learner in a group about main ideas can serve next as a teacher of the same skill to another group or can teach a different skill.

Name _____

PLANNING AN INTERVIEW

1. Write the subject of your report. (Example: Summer Fun)

MY Subject: _____

Now write a main idea (topic) sentence. (Example: In the summertime, you can have special kinds of fun right around your own neighborhood.)

MY Topic Sentence: _____

_____

2. Confer with some classmates. List two or more people you might interview to get information about your topic. (Examples: my grandmother, who grew up here in the city; Mr. Ramirez, our city's Park Recreation Director; my neighbor, Ms. McKew, who runs a day-camp for kids)

People I Want to Interview: _____

_____

_____

_____

3. Write some questions you'll ask during your interview. (Examples: What activities and games were part of your summer when you were a little kid? How does the Parks Department provide summer activities for kids and their families? Who can sign up for summer day-camp? What do campers do?)

MY Questions:

_____

_____

_____

_____

_____

_____

_____

_____

Name _____

BEFORE-AND-AFTER INTERVIEW CHECKLIST

1. Ahead of time:
  • I contacted the person I wish to interview.   Yes _____ No _____
  • I explained my purpose for the interview.   Yes _____ No _____
  • I set up an appointment for the interview.   Yes _____ No _____

The interview will take place at (time) _____(day, date) _____

(place) _____

  • I got permission to use a tape recorder/camera.   Yes _____ No _____

  • I have all the materials I need for the interview.   Yes _____ No _____

  • my main questions, each one written
    on a separate sheet of paper   Yes _____ No _____

  • pencils and pens   Yes _____ No _____

  • other supplies such as a tape recorder   Yes _____ No _____

2. After the interview:
  • I thanked the interviewee for sharing
    time and ideas with me.   Yes _____ No _____

  • I asked the interviewee to review my notes
    with me to make sure they are accurate.   Yes _____ No _____

  • I asked permission to contact the
    interviewee later if I have further
    questions.   Yes _____ No _____

3. Another tip:
After you write and publish your report, give a copy of it to each person you interviewed.
Interviewees appreciate seeing how their ideas have helped you, the writer.

A SAMPLE OUTLINE

(Report Subject:)

MAMMALS OF THE SEA

(Topic Sentence)
Earth's oceans are home to many fascinating and beautiful mammals.

(First Main Idea)
I. Ways Sea and Land Mammals Are Alike

(Facts)
A. Take in oxygen from the air

B. Nourish young with milk

C. Have hair, or hairlike structures

(Second Main Idea)
II. Examples of Sea Mammals and Their Behavior

(Facts)
A. Manatees: rise to surface to breathe

B. Dolphins: care for young for several years

C. Sea otters: thick fur insulates their bodies

(Final Idea)
III. Ways in Which Sea Mammals Are Threatened

(Facts)
A. Pollution of ocean water and air

Name _____

AN OUTLINE OF MY REPORT

Write the subject of your report:

_____

Draft a possible topic sentence:

_____

_____

(First Main Idea)

I. _____

_____

(Supporting Facts)

A. _____

B. _____

C. _____

(Second Main Idea)

II. _____

_____

(Supporting Facts)

A. _____

B. _____

C. _____

(Final Idea)

III. _____

(Supporting Facts)

A. _____

B. _____

C. _____

CONFERENCE CHECKLIST

Writer's Name: _____   **Partner's Name:** _____

Writer's Subject: _____

	Yes	No	Suggestions
1. The report sticks to the subject.			
2. There is a clear topic sentence at the beginning.			
3. The report develops the subject through one of these methods: examples, comparison and contrast, cause and effect, definition and example.			
4. The report has at least two paragraphs, each one developing a main idea about the subject.			
5. The writer has used several sources of information and has mentioned those sources.			

Other questions for partners to discuss:
- Who is the audience for this report?
- Is one of the first sentences a "hook" to get the audience interested? Does the report connect ideas by using helpful words and phrases like *in addition, as an example, the second step is..., because of that...* ?
- Would pictures or charts help readers understand the writer's subject? If so, has the writer supplied them?

NOTES